POINTERS FOR PARENTING FOR MENTAL HEALTH SERVICE PROFESSIONALS

POINTERS FOR PARENTING FOR MENTAL HEALTH SERVICE PROFESSIONALS

Rajinder M. Gupta, Ph.D.
Honorary Tutor, Birmingham University
Child and Adolescent Psychologist, Birmingham
Children's Hospital NHS Trust

and

Frederika C. Theus, Psy.D.
Clinical Psychologist, University of Illinois at Chicago

John Wiley & Sons, Ltd

Telephone (+44) 1243 779777
Email (for orders and customer service enquiries): cs-books@wiley.co.uk
Visit our Home Page on www.wiley.com

Clip art in Chapters 6 and 7 © 2006 Microsoft

Other Wiley Editorial Offices

John Wiley & Sons Inc., 111 River Street, Hoboken, NJ 07030, USA

Jossey-Bass, 989 Market Street, San Francisco, CA 94103-1741, USA

Wiley-VCH Verlag GmbH, Boschstr. 12, D-69469 Weinheim, Germany

John Wiley & Sons Australia Ltd, 42 McDougall Street, Milton, Queensland 4064, Australia

John Wiley & Sons (Asia) Pte Ltd, 2 Clementi Loop #02-01, Jin Xing Distripark, Singapore 129809

John Wiley & Sons Canada Ltd, 22 Worcester Road, Etobicoke, Ontario, Canada M9W 1L1

Wiley also publishes its books in a variety of electronic formats. Some content that appears in print
may not be available in electronic books.

Library of Congress Cataloging-in-Publication Data

Gupta, Rajinder M., 1939–
    Pointers for parenting for mental health service professionals /
Rajinder M. Gupta, and Frederika C. Theus.
        p.   cm.
    Includes bibliographical references and index.
    ISBN-13: 978-0-470-01938-2 (pbk. : alk. paper)
    ISBN-10: 0-470-01938-7 (pbk. : alk. paper)
  1. Parents–Services for.   2. Family psychotherapy.   3. Parenting.
4. Community Health Services.   5. Public health.   I. Theus, Frederika C.
II. Title.

RC488.5.G86 2006
616.89′156–dc22
                                            2005030792

British Library Cataloguing in Publication Data

A catalogue record for this book is available from the British Library

ISBN-10 0-470-01938-7 (pbk)
ISBN-13 978-0-470-01938-2 (pbk)

Typeset in 10/12pt Palatino by SNP Best-set Typesetter Ltd., Hong Kong
Printed and bound in Great Britain by TJ International, Padstow, Cornwall
This book is printed on acid-free paper responsibly manufactured from sustainable forestry in which
at least two trees are planted for each one used for paper production.

CONTENTS

ABOUT THE AUTHORS

Rajinder M. Gupta studied psychology at the universities of Cambridge and Manchester. He did his professional training as an educational psychologist at Exeter University and PhD at Aston. Following his training, he worked as an educational psychologist for nearly two decades. In the last 15 years, he has worked as a Child and Adolescent Psychologist in the clinical psychology departments of several NHS trusts in the Midlands and has also helped train a number of clinical psychology trainees studying for their doctorate programme at Birmingham University. His current main area of interest, both from a clinical and academic standpoint, is the study of families with interactional difficulties with their children and effective and efficient ways of helping them.

Also by Rajinder M. Gupta

Gupta RM & Coxhead P (eds) *Cultural Diversity and Learning Efficiency: Recent Developments in Assessment*, London: Macmillan, 1988.

Gupta RM & Coxhead P (eds) *Intervention with Children*, London: Routledge, 1990.

Gupta RM & Coxhead P (eds) *Asesoramiento y Apoyo Psicopedagogico*, Madrid: Narcea, 1993. (Translation of a revision of *Intervention with Children.*)

Gupta DS & Gupta RM (eds) *Psychology for Psychiatrists*, London: Whurr Publishers, 2000.

Gupta R & Parry-Gupta D (ed.) *Children and Parents. Clinical Issues for Psychologists and Psychiatrists*, London: Whurr Publishers, 2003.

Frederika C. Theus is a licensed clinical psychologist and coordinator of the Child and Adolescent Diagnostic and Family Support Program for the Family Clinic, Institute on Disability and Human Development at the University of Illinois at Chicago. She provides evaluations for children with suspected or previously diagnosed developmental disabilities as part of a multidisciplinary team. Dr Theus also provides therapy and intervention services to children, adolescents, and adults with developmental disabilities, including autism and Asperger Syndrome. Dr Theus received a Master of Arts degree in Learning Disabilities from Northwestern University, and worked as both a diagnostician and as a Learning Disabilities teacher. She earned her doctorate in psychology from the Illinois School of Professional Psychology. Dr Theus provides workshops and trainings to parents and professionals on a variety of topics related to assessment and intervention for individuals with developmental disabilities, including dual diagnosis of developmental disabilities and mental health disorders, behavioural intervention, and Asperger Syndrome. She has published on topics related to child development. Dr Theus is a member of the professional advisory committee for the Autism Society of Illinois and the advisory council of the Chicago Southside Autism Support Group.

PREFACE AND OVERVIEW OF THE BOOK

Pointers for Parenting for Mental Health Service Professionals will be of practical help to trainees, recently qualified professionals working in Child and Adolescent Mental Health Service (CAMHS) teams when they are doing their child placements, and professionals who routinely work with children and families. This is because the book has developed as a result of actual hands-on experience of working with parents and children in clinical set-ups over a number of years. More importantly, our belief that this book will be of benefit to the aforementioned professionals has been borne out by the comments of colleagues who have very kindly read it during draft stages.

In this book, wherever possible, we have tried to illustrate our point, or a theoretical issue, with one or more cases, as necessary. They are all real cases in which we ourselves[1] have actually been involved over the years. Where appropriate, on a few occasions, the same case has been used more than once. For the sake of confidentiality, obviously, we have changed the subjects' real names. When we have given details, in nearly all cases we have not stated how we dealt with the case or what the outcome was, because we feel that this is not intended to be a case study book per se, where a case history is given followed by the strategies used to deal with the problem and finally what the outcome was. Instead, what this book offers is outlined in the next few pages.

---

[1] Although the use of 'we' may give the appearance that the authors work together and see families together, this is not in fact the case. The word 'we' (in the majority of the situations) has been chosen simply because it seems more concise than using 'the first or second author'. We should also add that the majority of cases to which we have alluded in the text are from the UK.

OVERVIEW OF THE BOOK

The introductory chapter attempts to give the flavour of the book and describes the thinking that underpins it. In Chapter 2, some of the topics that we address include the stressful and demanding nature of bringing up children, which can result in many parents feeling guilty, bewildered, depressed, unhappy, not knowing what to do, and so on. John McEnroe, the celebrated tennis champion and father of six children, who has been married twice, has said 'it's made me understand that there is no tougher job in the world than being a good parent' (cited in *The Observer*, 22 May 2004). We share McEnroe's view in this respect in that it captures the enormity of the responsibility that parents have in bringing up children.

Another topic that frequently crops up in our consultations is the attributional error that many parents unintentionally make. Under this topic, we have attempted to categorise the parents that clinicians[2] often see during their practice. These categories are neither discrete nor exhaustive. They are the ones which clinicians are more likely to come across in their routine practice. We hope that those clinicians, either in training, or with relatively less clinical experience, who may not have had the opportunities of coming across such a range of different types of parents that we have detailed here and the type of attributional errors they make, should benefit from the description and some of their reactions that we have provided in this book. Armed with this information, clinicians may then tailor their intervention accordingly. For instance, there are a very small percentage of parents one sees in a clinic set-up who continually put up barriers or fail to implement any advice given. Then there are parents who tend to medicalise the problem when it is essentially of a psychological nature; there are some parents who think that it is the child who needs 'treatment' and totally reject the importance of bi-directionality, i.e. how the child's behaviour is influenced by the parents' behaviour and vice versa. Frankly, with such parents, the advice embodied in the form of the pointers just does not work. In such cases little change can be expected in the family dynamics unless they can be successfully engaged. But these types of parents are only in the minority. The majority of parents do try to implement these strategies and are successful in resolving problems or being able to cope in a much better way. Finally, we also look at topics often reported in child development books, such as parenting styles and the effect they can have on the children's development.

---

[2] 'Clinician'/'therapist': these terms refer to various professionals who work in child and adolescent mental health services teams. These include psychiatrists of various grades, psychotherapists, occupational therapists, social workers, clinical psychologists, and so on.

In Chapter 3, we address some of the topics frequently raised by parents during our consultations with them. These include topics like bi-directionality, nature versus nurture; why it is virtually impossible for clinicians to tell parents with any certainty which factor or factors could be impinging on their children's behaviour – which is something that parents want clinicians to identify when they come to see them; parents having unrealistic expectations of their children in terms of their behaviours which are not commensurate with their age, cognitive and emotional development, aptitude, and so on: when that happens, it can lead to serious interactional difficulties between children and their parents as children are not able to meet their parents' expectations.

These are not just theoretical issues but important topics which have a tremendous bearing on the way the parents see the problems of their children and on possible solutions. We have tried to incorporate these topics from the point of view of their clinical usefulness and relevance rather than just as esoteric academic subject matter and to treat these topics accordingly. A mother who thinks that her child is behaving aggressively and violently in the same way as the child's father may come to therapy sessions believing that any therapeutic process is unlikely to bring about any change because their child has inherited those characteristics and therefore may not be amenable to any modification. In our view, before a clinician embarks on any intervention programme, such issues need to be addressed first with convincing evidence, and parents need to be helped to revise their views about such matters. It is this logic (and because they are raised by so many parents and so often) that has been a determining factor in our deciding to include them in this chapter.

Chapter 4 serves two functions. First, it introduces some preliminary issues before we go on to describe some general pointers. We consider the preliminary issues to be important, even if many of them may appear obvious. Their significance lies in the fact that, to a certain extent, success or failure of the pointers in bringing about any change in family functioning does depend upon them. To give a flavour of their importance, consider the following brief outline of one of the preliminary points:

'The first thing that needs to be stated quite unequivocally is that parents need to be willing, determined, motivated and consistent to implement these pointers to draw any real benefit from them. Trying them half-heartedly is not going to bring about any desirable results. They need to try these with an open mind. While these pointers are not claimed to be a panacea, having tried and tested them we can say with confidence that these are effective and they do help bring about changes in the child's behaviour and the family dynamics where parents have *implemented* them.'

This is obvious but it is essential both for the clinician and for the parent to be aware of it. Where parents do not implement any suggestions given and continue with the status quo (i.e. persist with unsuccessful management strategies that have not worked in the past), it is hardly likely that any improvement in the child's behaviour is going to take place. This situation is not dissimilar to continuing to take medicine that has clearly not worked previously; if one still carries on with it, it is not going to cure or ameliorate the problem. This analogy is true not just about our pointers but about any intervention strategy, i.e. if it is not implemented, parents are unlikely to see any change/improvement in their child's presenting problems.

After these preliminary points, we go on to describe some pointers in this chapter and, where apposite, they are illustrated with reference to a case study (or case studies). We describe some of these pointers at considerable length and include areas like 'looking after oneself', 'helping children with homework', 'realistic expectations', and so on. Most of the pointers in Chapter 4 have been dealt with in greater detail than those in Chapter 5. We happen to think that the ones we have treated at length in Chapter 4 merit that type of treatment. Had we placed all the pointers in one chapter it would have made that chapter far too long. Thus Chapter 5 has the remaining pointers, some of which are quite brief. For instance: undesirable behaviours should not be rewarded by unwittingly giving in, or by starting to pay attention to the child when he[3] is misbehaving.

Chapter 6 provides the details of our adapted and acceptable behaviour modification approach. Our rationale for including this chapter in a book where the thrust is to deal with positive pointers for parenting is that our therapeutic approach which we have described here is an important part of the pointers that we have developed. For instance, before we came across any literature supportive of our views (see Rhodes, 2003, cited in Hastings and Beck, 2004), we repeatedly observed that if parents are stressed, their ability to implement any therapeutic intervention becomes seriously impaired. In view of this, if we consider that during our initial assessment parents are highly stressed because of their children's behaviours and other factors in their lives, our advice to them invariably is that their stress levels need to be addressed first and reduced. By tackling it first, we have often found that this can have an indirect positive effect on their children's behaviours and the quality of family interactions. In fact, in one case, while we were carrying out a 'screening assessment' of a family to determine whether ours was the right service for them, the mother of the referred child became acutely aware that she was highly

---

[3] 'He': the authors have used 'he' to refer inclusively to both boys and girls, instead of using the more unwieldy phrase 'he or she'.

stressed due to various things that were going on in her life. The additional problems of her son were just the last straw.

Given the aims of our screening assessment, the problems of her stress were not pursued, except to acknowledge it, and to point out how it can play quite a critical role in the way we interact with our children under these circumstances. However, after a few weeks, the family was seen for the purposes of therapeutic intervention. During the course of the first session, this mother reported that there had been '70 per cent improvement' since the 'screening'. We were somewhat surprised as to how such an improvement had taken place in such a short space of time and without any help for her child's chronic behaviour problem from any source. When we asked this mother about this dramatic improvement, she explained that the screening assessment made her aware how stressed she generally felt. It also made her realise how her being so stressed most of the time could be having a profound effect on the way she treated her son. This led her to realise further that it was perhaps the way she treated her son that was having an adverse effect on his behaviour. As a result of this awareness, she took active steps to reduce her stress level, and in so doing, it changed the way she handled her son, and this in turn improved his behaviour substantially. Rhodes (2003, cited in Hastings & Beck, 2004) not only echoes our views but describes our actual clinical practice when he states that: 'behavioural intervention for severe problem behaviour in children with intellectual disabilities [we would add that the nature of the disability is not critical] is most successful when family issues including stress have been addressed pre-intervention' (p. 1339). Our adapted behaviour modification approach takes parental stress into account and offers strategies to deal with it.

To a certain extent, in Chapter 6 and elsewhere (see Coxhead & Gupta, 1989; Gupta & Coxhead, 1990; Gupta & Parry-Gupta, 2003), we have outlined our reasoning, supported by a considerable body of research, as to why, over the years, we have felt it necessary to adapt behaviour modification, which is a highly researched and well-established therapeutic intervention.

We have called our last chapter 'From pointers to practice'. In this chapter, what we have tried to do is briefly to outline parental responses to our pointers and our therapeutic approach in general and its effectiveness. At one end of the spectrum, we have a substantial number of parents who have implemented the advice given. With this group of parents we have found that our approach and pointers are effective. At the other end of the spectrum, we have parents who are always putting up barriers to whatever is suggested; with such a group of parents, our approach is less successful. In addition to these two categories of parents, we have also outlined responses to other categories of parents, e.g. those whose cases are horrendously complex, those who are inconsistent, those who have differences in parenting style, and so on. We do not regard these categories as discrete and you may notice that there are overlaps.

We have tried to make the book accessible; it is therefore anticipated that these professionals would be able to recommend it to parents so that the pointers in this book can serve as a reminder of what was discussed during the consultation session. Alternatively, clinicians may choose to photocopy the pointers that have been discussed and explained during the clinical session and give them to the parents at the end of the session, or send them by post. Our experience shows that many parents often find this practice very helpful, and we expand on this point later in the book.

In the present climate of evidence-based practice, we must acknowledge that neither our pointers nor our adapted behaviour modification approach are based on any empirical evidence per se. However, what we can say with substantial confidence is that what we are offering in this book stems from our more than two decades of clinical experience; in addition, it is also based on a balanced mixture of relevant theory and practice. More crucially, in our clinical judgement, our pointers and our adapted behaviour modification approach are effective in helping to improve a vast majority of children's behaviours and the 'parent/child dyadic mutuality' (Deater-Deckard & Petrill, 2004); and parents, on the whole, do not put up barriers in accepting and implementing them. We consider this to be the strength, and perhaps uniqueness, of this book.

ACKNOWLEDGEMENTS

We have been greatly privileged that a few colleagues and academic friends very kindly read this book at the draft stage and made some very helpful and constructive comments. We would particularly like to mention Dr Sara De Costa who was able to give us some feedback not only from the point of view of a clinical psychologist but also from the perspective of a mother. In the latter role it was very heartening for us to know that Sara's views about the effectiveness of these pointers, and their acceptance by a vast number of families in real situations, were in accord with our experience of using them. As well as receiving views from colleagues, experienced and recently qualified, academic psychologists, we also had some very helpful comments from trainee clinical psychologists who tried to implement some of these pointers while they were with us during their child speciality placements. Another colleague we feel we should mention by name is Tara Hickey, MA, Assistant Psychologist, who very generously not only proofread the whole book but also made some very helpful suggestions. We are happy to note that, in the main, their responses have been positive and encouraging about the usefulness and effectiveness of these pointers in the management of children's behaviours and also in improving the quality of relationships between parents and children. The encouraging comments that we have received from a range of professionals who read, and some of whom implemented the pointers, have influenced and encouraged us to transform these ideas into this present book. We are most grateful to all of them for their time and valued comments.

Last, but not least, many thanks to Rajinder Gupta's son, Rahul, who with his computer skills was able to help his father on numerous occasions.

Rajinder M. Gupta
Frederika C. Theus

1

INTRODUCTION

The inspiration of this book stems from actually working with children and families who were often referred to the Child and Adolescent Mental Health Services (CAMHS) for psychological/psychiatric intervention. Our ideas about this book started to evolve more than a decade ago. During the early stages of gestation of this book, we were influenced by some of the research that showed that most patients forget, almost immediately, the majority of information given to them by their family doctors when they go to visit them. McGuire (1996) found that 40–80% of the medical information provided is forgotten immediately and the amount of information correctly recalled is also surprisingly small (Goodwin, 2000; see also Kessels, 2003, for other aspects of patients' ability to retain medical information). This led us to realise that it was likely that something similar could happen in the consultations offered by CAMHS professionals/clinicians, despite the differences in the practising style of the members of these two professions. Our sessions often last much longer and perhaps we give a lot more information to our clients than a typical family doctor.

Here is an example of our giving information to the mother of a five-year-old boy, Luke, born prematurely at 25 weeks, who had a number of complications during the first three years of his life. Luke's mother, Mrs S, also had a lot of physical problems: she suffered from acute arthritis and the 'bottom half' of her body had loose joints. She was often in and out of hospital to relieve her of pain. In one year, she was admitted to hospital three times. When she was in hospital or was unwell, Luke was looked after by his grandmother. Mrs S also suffered from kidney failure.

The reason for Luke's referral was that he had become aggressive and violent towards his mother. Luke had always been hyperactive even when he was ill, and his behaviour problems occurred almost every day, as reported by his mother. Mrs S wondered if Luke had Asperger's Syndrome and whether his behaviour problems might be related to that. When Luke was seen in the clinic situation, he displayed no symptoms which are commonly associated with Asperger's Syndrome, e.g. impairment in social interaction or repetitive patterns of behaviour, and the pattern of his language development did not resemble that which is typically observed in children with this condition. Our formulation was that Luke's behaviour problems were chiefly due to the fact that inappropriate patterns of behaviours were unwittingly reinforced by his mother in the home environment. Luke's school report showed that his behaviour in school was acceptable, when he was receiving appropriate attention.

Based on Luke's history, and our formulation of the problem, Mrs S was given the following advice. Each point was carefully explained in detail. Here we won't expand on the rationale which underpins the advice which we gave to Mrs S, as all these points are taken up later in the book and fully explained.

1. As a result of Luke and Mrs S's medical conditions, it was easier for his mother to give in to even his unreasonable demands. Luke, in view of this, learnt that if he persevered with his demands, his mother would give in. This led us to explain to Mrs S how behaviour is learnt, according to the learning theory, and this included explaining the concepts of antecedent, behaviour, consequence (ABC).
2. Saying 'yes' in the first place if she feels she is going to say yes eventually.
3. What psychologists mean by ignoring undesirable behaviour.
4. Holding Luke when he tries to hit and hurt his mother.
5. Positively reinforcing desirable behaviour.
6. How children's behaviour can cause a lot of stress to parents and what they can do about it.

We consider that the above advice is substantially more than what one is likely to receive when one visits one's GP or sees a consultant. Hence, it can be quite difficult to retain all the information that we sometimes give to our families. Furthermore, it can sometimes also happen that the information or advice we give may be emotive, and parents and families may even be actively blocking what was said (cf. Wessel et al., 2000). Therefore, it was reasonable to speculate that the clients who saw CAMHS professionals also forgot a considerable amount of information following the session.

It is important that the advice given to the families is retained and implemented. Obviously, if they forget half of it – and some of it could be quite critical – it is then likely that the intervention offered may not be very effective. The significance of accurately retaining the information given can be illustrated by the case history of Laura, a fourteen-year-old grammar school girl. We explained the concept of home-based reinforcement (for details of this model, see Gupta & Coxhead, 1990) to her head of year to deal with Laura's difficulties. Part of this intervention strategy was that, if Laura exhibited the agreed behaviour in class, the teacher would reinforce it at the end of her lesson by both verbal praise and by written feedback in the form of a presentable card. (A special card was devised for this purpose where the teacher was able to indicate whether or not the individual concerned managed to reach the desirable level of behaviour in class. This card was then taken home to be presented to her parents.) On giving her parents this card, Laura was expected to receive a small reward, previously agreed by herself and her parents.

It was the teacher's responsibility to see Laura at the end of the lesson, praise her for her good behaviour and give her the mutually agreed card to take home. This feedback card contained information on whether Laura had managed to behave in the class. It was not for Laura to have to go to her teacher and ask if her behaviour had reached the desirable level. Unfortunately, the teacher *misremembered* the verbal information given and instead expected Laura to go and ask her at the end of each lesson if she had been happy with her behaviour. Laura did not go to her teacher to ask about it. She was a very sensitive girl, lacking in confidence, and felt too embarrassed to go and ask her teacher about her behaviour at the end of each lesson. As Laura never went and asked the teacher, she therefore never received any verbal praise or the agreed card from her teacher to take home, even when she did behave and showed a significant improvement in her behaviour in class. Consequently, she was unable to provide the required information/evidence to her parents that she had been behaving better in her class. Laura's parents never gave her any reward, all the time assuming erroneously that Laura's behaviour in school was no better than before. She persevered and behaved better for some time but eventually gave up, as her desirable behaviour, instead of being reinforced, was being ignored. This is just one example that illustrates that it is important on the part of the person receiving psychological advice that its key aspects are remembered for it to be successful in bringing about the desirable change. When that happens, not only does the undesirable behaviour not change but people who are using psychological therapies stop believing in their effectiveness and give up.

Having become aware of these problems as to how people can so easily forget the information given verbally, and with a view to overcoming this, we started to try out the following two approaches. Either all the key management points discussed during the consultation session were written down briefly on a piece of paper and given to the parents at the end of the session or we sent them a letter after the visit as a reminder of the essential management points discussed when they were seen. For instance, the points discussed could have been:

- ignore trivial behaviours where the child is not hurting himself or anybody else but is just being irritating;

- reward desirable behaviours;
- feeling guilty does not help.

During the session with the parents, each of these points would be discussed in considerable detail to ensure that they fully understood them and their relevance to the referred problem was carefully explained. Also, during the beginning of our next session, we would often go over the points to ensure that parents still remembered them and that their ramifications were still clear to them. There is some evidence to suggest that when advice is presented in written form it leads to 'better treatment adherence' (Blinder, Rotenberg, Peleg & Taicher, 2001; Kessels, 2003).

We have received very positive feedback from the parents about this practice. They found that the pointers acted as an aide-memoire for them and made it slightly easier for them to implement the advice given. This also helped to avoid the type of misunderstanding that we have alluded to above in the short case study of Laura. As a result of this practice, over the years we have managed to build up a whole list of such pointers, which is the main raison d'être of this book.

This book does assume some basic knowledge of many topics related to child development on the part of the clinicians. However, some topics have been briefly delineated where appropriate and where, more importantly, they have been the subject of discussion with many families. An example of the latter is imitation in children. Sometimes some parents have asked us, 'Why are children selective in what they imitate?' For example, they may imitate only a small number of the many acts that they have observed. There are a few hypotheses as to whether the child will or will not imitate what they have observed. In the act of imitation, a number of processes are implicated and that imitation serves different functions at different stages of the child's development. For this reason, the motivation to imitate at two years old will be different from that at age six or 15.

Children are likely to imitate if what they observe does not appear too difficult to copy. In one experiment, many two-year-old children stopped playing, they protested, clung to their mother, and cried after seeing the experimenter display actions that were difficult for them to understand or remember well (Kagan, 1981). On the other hand, children did not show any distress when the actions that were shown to them were easy to imitate. This information can be used to explain to the parents in response to their question that if what children observe appears too difficult to imitate, they are unlikely to copy it, and it is one of the reasons why whatever children observe they do not necessarily imitate.

Next follows an example where we expect clinicians to have some familiarity with child development issues. As many clinicians know, many parents often have expectations of their children's behaviours, which are not always realistic and not commensurate with their age and ability (cf. Chess & Thomas, 1999). With some knowledge and understanding of child development issues, clinician can advise parents whether their children are capable of showing the type of behaviour that they are expecting or whether they need to revise their expectations in the light of the child's development. When we discuss the issue of realistic expectations later in the book, we give a number of examples where we felt parents' expectations were not commensurate with the child's ability, age, and aptitude. However, it is not possible for us to cover each and every possible eventuality about the child's behaviour and say which expectation, and what age, on the part of the parent, is appropriate and which is not. What we have done is to draw clinicians' attention to this important topic, which has frequently occurred in our practice; it would then be up to the clinician to offer an opinion when parents raise their concerns, whether their expectations are in line with the child's development levels. What we can say here – and we address this issue at some considerable length again later in the book – is that it is an important issue. Very frequently parents have unrealistic expectations of their children's behaviours and very often it is one of the main reasons as to why many parents have conflicts with their children. It often proves to be an important barrier to positive parenting.

2

CHILDREN AND PARENTS: SOME GENERAL CONSIDERATIONS

INTRODUCTION

It is hardly controversial to say that a vast majority of parents love their children. It is also true to say that a huge majority of them know – and experience the fact – that bringing up children is stressful, demanding, frustrating, disappointing, irritating, and anxiety provoking (and perhaps sometimes fun!). This view about children and parents, and the effect that children's behaviour can have on their parents, has been formed as a result of our dealing with a somewhat skewed population, i.e. on the basis of hundreds of families that we have seen in clinic situations and who have been referred to our services by various agencies for one problem or another.

A very high proportion of the families who are referred to Child and Adolescent Mental Health Services (CAMHS) often have very complex problems and are in difficult circumstances: financial, court battles with their partners, problems arising from being reconstituted due to marriage breakdowns, mental illness, lack of any social support, living in very 'rough areas' and so on. All this is further compounded by the problems of their children. Consider the following schematic representation of Michael's family, their complex circumstances, and their number of sources of stresses which are impacting on their family lives. We are sure that, besides the sources that we have identified with the family's help, there are a number of other areas in their lives which also produce stress on them (see Figure 2.1).

Michael's is not the only family which experiences stress from a variety of sources. Hinsliff (2004) reported the case of a stressed teacher who arrived at her school wearing her bedroom slippers. She said to the *Observer* reporter, Hinsliff: 'I was aware that the wheels were coming

Family Stresses

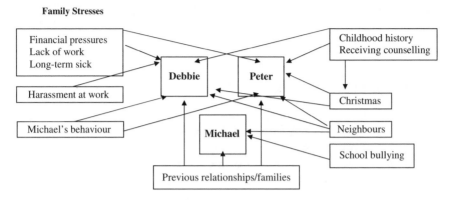

Figure 2.1 Sources of stress on Michael's parents

off . . . I was in a full-time job, full-on job and torn between maintaining that, and my children, and my house, and my relationship with my husband. Everything was giving way' (p. 19). There is burgeoning evidence in the literature (e.g. Berg-Nielsen, Vika & Dahl, 2003; Crnic & Acevedo, 1995; Pelham & Lang, 1999; Sidebotham, 2001 and several studies cited later in the book) which highlights how families experience pressures for diverse reasons, and bringing up children is an additional factor, particularly if the child has emotional or behavioural difficulties. A recent 'Practitioner Review' by Hastings & Beck (2004) cites several studies which have shown that parents with children who have intellectual disabilities suffer from a lot more parenting stress than parents of children without disabilities. Sometimes, because of the cumulative effect of the families' problems, and the stress arising from them, it adversely affects parents' social lives and mental well-being (see also Donenberg & Baker, 1993; Galboda-Liyanage, Prince & Scott, 2003).

A 21-year-old single mother said to us that she had been on medication for one month because of her feeling depressed and due to panic attacks. She felt that the total effect of her 45-year-old mother's death due to breast cancer, her three-year-old son's behaviour problems exacerbated due to his autism, and having to deal with her son's brain operations, were all too much for her to cope with single-handed. On top of all that, she had lost all her social support: her friends did not want to know her because they were afraid that she would burden them with her problems.

The feelings and experiences of many parents about their children, as described above, become even worse, and more intense, when they feel that they are almost out of their control and whatever they do with them, nothing seems to work. Consider the impact on any parent of the following behaviours at home of a 13-year-old girl, Penny, with moderate learning difficulties. These were reported to us by her mother, her aunt and her cousin, when they came to see us.

- Penny talked about sex a lot; she seemed to be fixated with it.
- She had broken the lock of the door.
- She had cut the phone wire in anger.
- She had hit her mother with a fork.
- She had tipped tea all over the house.
- She often said to her parents that they could not 'touch her'; if they did, she would report them to the social services.
- Her parents tried various punishments to no effect. When they sent Penny to her bedroom, she climbed out of her bedroom window and went out with her friends often drinking, sometimes using drugs. She came home when she wanted to – which was often at about eleven at night.

Penny's mother said that her husband found it very difficult to cope with her daughter's undesirable behaviours and as a result had started having panic attacks. Of the many children referred to CAMHS teams, up and down the country, some are obviously worse than Penny and the behaviour of some is not bad as hers. As many clinicians would know, the range of problems presented by children is often very varied.

Age is no barrier for children to present problems to parents or for parents to have problems with them, irrespective of their age. For instance, a six-month-old baby may present problems by not sleeping through the night. Thus a parent can have disturbed sleep for months on end. A three-year-old child may throw many 'wobblies' whenever his parents take him out. A ten-year-old child may present problems by often being defiant, moody, constantly making demands for things parents can ill afford, being aggressive towards younger siblings and so on. Young adolescents' problems could include: staying out late, playing music loud in the house, getting drunk, and generally having an attitude problem. If these problems are not handled appropriately, chances are that in time they will get worse rather than better.

Although the nature of these problems may be different, their effect on parents can be very draining. A single mother of a 12-year-old boy, Stephen, who had been expelled from school, said to us that we did not understand what an awful effect her son's behaviour was having on her. It depressed her and made her feel like self-harming by slashing her wrists. Several times she entertained the idea of walking out of the house and having her children taken into care by the social services. Sometimes, children's difficult behaviours can have a grave effect on marital relationships, which can add further stress to the total family dynamics. In fact, Stephen's mother said that her husband left her the previous year because of Stephen's bad behaviour. It was too much for him and he just could not cope with it. Constant clashes between 15-year-old John and his mother resulted in his parents having to live separately. John's father said that they had no option but to take such a drastic step, because living together was like living in hell. The only way, the parents felt, that they could maintain their sanity was that, of their children, two stayed with their mother and John lived separately with his father. This was their plan – at least for the foreseeable future.

PARENTAL INTERPRETATIONS OF CHILDREN'S DIFFICULTIES

Attribution Errors

When parents are experiencing a whole gamut of problems with their children, not only do they observe and experience their consequences, they also try to understand the possible underlying reasons. For instance, parents want to know why and what make their children have an attitude problem; or, what makes them aggressive towards them; or why is their child so clingy? Fourteen-year-old Ben's mother, divorced, mother of three children, wanted to know why her son never does as he is told and always wants to have his own way. Thirteen-year-old Layla's mother wanted to determine why her daughter won't let her have her own life as well. When we are engaged in such a process of finding out, what we are then trying to do is to 'attribute' a cause or causes to that event or happening. In so doing, we try to use available information to make inferences about the root of a particular behaviour (Clarke, 1996, p. 9). While we may make an attempt to attribute a cause or causes to an event or incident, it does not necessarily follow that we are right. When we are wrong in ascribing right cause(s), this is described as an 'attribution error' (for a review of the literature, see Miller, 1995; see also Bolton et al., 2003, who add a different dimension to the issue of attribution, expressed emotion and mental illness in mothers). Often, when parents make an attribution error, they underestimate the influence of situational factors in explaining the behaviour, and over-emphasise the importance of dispositional or child-centred factors. In the next few pages, we illustrate this by a number of case studies under two main headings: medicalising and abnormalising the problem, and other factors as the underlying cause.

The way parents think about the child's behaviour often influences the way they behave towards them. For instance, if a parent thinks that the child is complaining because he is always moaning, he is likely to receive little sympathy. If, on the other hand, a parent thinks that their child was complaining because he was unwell, under these circumstances he is likely to get a lot more sympathy and a parent would perhaps be more patient with him as well. Obviously, over the long term, the way parents behave towards their children has a bearing on the way children develop (Miller, 1995). The following familiar lines, though not strictly based on any empirical evidence, describe how different types of parental behaviours can have an effect on the personality of children.

Children Learn What They Live
If a child lives with *criticism* he learns to *criticise*.
If a child lives with *hostility*, he learns to *fight*.
If a child lives with *ridicule*, he learns to be *shy*.
If a child lives with *shame*, he learns to feel *guilty*.
If a child lives with *tolerance*, he learns to be *patient*.
If a child lives with *encouragement*, he learns *confidence*.
If a child lives with *praise*, he learns to *appreciate*.
If a child lives with *security*, he learns to have *faith*.
If a child lives with *approval*, he learns to *like himself*.
If a child lives with *acceptance* and *friendship*, he learns to find *love in the world*.

Medicalising and Abnormalising the Problem

It is not uncommon for a number of parents we see to attribute the cause of their child's problem to some underlying pathology. In line with this thinking, some parents become fully convinced that what their child needs is some medication and not psychological input and guidance to help deal with the child's problems. Sometimes it is done overtly, and in certain cases, by inference. We will address the former example first.

Take the case of Penny, mentioned above. She presented very serious behaviour problems both at home and at school and was virtually out of her parents' control. She completely ruled the roost, did whatever she wanted to do and did not care what she said to people. Penny asked the family support worker who went to see the family at home, in a manner wholly inappropriate to her age and ability, if she was gay because she had short hair. While it was almost impossible for Penny's parents to manage her, her aunt and cousin, whom she saw quite frequently could cope with her. Penny's cousin and aunt gave two reasons as to why Penny behaved the way she did with her parents, namely that her parents had always given in and that Penny was very attention seeking. Suggestion by other professionals that Penny's problems stemmed from the way her parents interacted with her were robustly rejected by her parents and they criticised the professionals, saying that they did not know what they were doing and talking about. Despite Penny's aunt's and cousin's views, and other professionals' assessments, her parents did not accept that the way they dealt with Penny's behaviours could be a critical factor in the way she behaved. Penny's mother felt very strongly that there was something medically wrong with Penny and wanted her to have a blood test and brain scan. In the circumstances, the case was referred back to their family doctor, as Penny's parents did not think that psychological intervention was going to be of much help.

Sometimes, parents bring along with them a friend or a relative, who they think has a similar physiological based problem to that of their own child. Often such a person is used by parents to back up their own views about the aetiology of their child's problems. Some parents tend to have greater confidence in their friend's diagnostic skills than in the expertise of the clinician. Such a friend or relative often asserts that in their opinion, based on their experience of their own child, the referred child has the same problem as their own.

Another example is where parents had looked up certain symptoms of a condition on the Internet and had tried to convince us that their child suffered from similar symptoms. In the case of a 12-year-old child with moderate learning difficulties, his mother first wanted to convince us that he had dyslexia because he displayed symptoms commonly associated with this condition. When her attention was drawn to the fact that he did not meet that criterion, she then wondered if he had ADHD. Again, when it was pointed out that he did not meet the DSM-IV criterion for us to diagnose him as suffering from ADHD, she started to suggest that he had autism. Finally, she wondered if her son was suffering from depression and was at a risk of self-harm.

ADHD is another condition frequently referred to these days by quite a few parents we see in the clinic situation to explain their child's difficulties. Many parents who believe that their child has ADHD 'tend to adopt a disease-model pattern of attributions . . . in comparison to parents of non-problem children' (Bugental & Johnston, 2000, p. 329). They attribute children's behaviours to internal causes, regard them as stable, and are convinced in their thinking that neither the child nor they can do anything about it; the only thing that can help is some kind of medication.

Sometimes medical problems being the cause of the child's difficulties are not overtly stated but are implied when parents describe the difficulties they are experiencing with their children. They tend to attribute those difficulties in their children to some underlying pathology, though they may not use any medical or psychiatric terminology to describe it. Wittingly or unwittingly, they make assiduous efforts to reject any suggestion by the clinician that the real basis of the child's difficulties could be due to the way they manage the child. Such parents tend to justify their reasoning by rationalising that their age gives them the benefit of being always right irrespective of the way they deal with their child's difficulties. Such parents often tend to believe that because a child is only a child, he must be wrong rather than themselves. Because they are the parents, they view themselves as older and wiser, and therefore they cannot be wrong. So, in the opinion of such parents, something has to be wrong with the child which accounts for his 'odd' behaviour. The following case study attempts to illustrate this point.

Oliver, an eight-year-old boy, was referred to us by his GP for being extremely difficult at home. This is how his mother expressed his difficulties to her GP. Oliver had frequent temper tantrums and cried and sulked at the slightest thing. He was very disobedient towards his mother. However, he got on all right at school; his teachers said that he was as good as gold and his mother should be proud of him. He did very well in his SAT results and won a colouring competition. He had a younger brother, aged six, who was described as a perfectly well-behaved boy. His mother (Mrs A) had been divorced for about five years but, according to her, difficulties between her and her ex-husband still persisted. Even after their divorce for five years, their solicitors were still involved in trying to sort out their battles. Mrs A completely blamed her husband for the marriage breakdown. On the other hand, Mrs A's parents were critical of her and felt that if she had really tried she could have saved her marriage and would not have been in such a mess. As they blamed her for her marriage breakdown, therefore, they provided little practical or emotional support to her. The only support she had was from one of her neighbours who was considerably older than her and with whom she had a good relationship. Mrs A said that she felt mildly depressed.

The two boys had regular access to their father but Mrs A felt that he had tried to poison their minds against her when they went and saw him. Mrs A kept herself extremely busy – from our point of view inordinately so – possibly trying to do far too many things. Consequently, she was under great stress, making her very short-tempered and impatient with her children. For instance, by the time of one of her appointments with us at 12.30, she had already attended four engagements including a dental appointment. After she had finished with us, she had lined up at least three more major jobs before the evening, following which she would need to attend to cooking, her children and routine household chores. On top of this, she was also doing a part-time degree in computer science.

Mrs A was of the opinion that something was pathologically wrong with her son; otherwise, he would not be constantly asking questions, getting bored very easily, moaning about petty things, never being happy, and being obsessive about keeping his room tidy. If he did not do as he was told straight away, his mother shouted at him a lot. This is despite the fact that Mrs A said that if she spoke softly to him, he did listen and did as he was told. When we saw him in the clinic, he kept himself busy and made no demands on his mother. He kept himself occupied with a couple of cars that he had borrowed from the clinic's toys collection. When we saw him in the clinic, his behaviour in that situation was perfectly within his age and ability range, except that he tended to be shy and did not engage in any dialogue with us. We saw absolutely nothing in his behaviour which we would deem as unacceptable. Given our own observations of his behaviour, and the information that we had from his school about his behaviour there, we tried to assure Mrs A that we did not see anything abnormal with his behaviour that would suggest a medical or psychological disorder. But that was not the answer she was looking for. What she really wanted from us was that we affirmed that something was medically/psychologically wrong with him; that the way she dealt with his behaviour problems was perfectly satisfactory from a psychological point of view. Obviously, we could not do that as we did not think that anything was wrong with Oliver.

Mrs A said that she had not been able to implement the advice given because she had been far too busy with other things including moving house. It was made plain to her that unless she implemented the advice, she could not expect any changes in Oliver's behaviour. At least at the time of writing this case study, she had not been able to accept that Oliver's unacceptable behaviour was largely due to the way she managed him and not due to any underlying pathology.

Another situation that frequently results in parents making attributional errors is when they find that shortly after displaying difficult behaviour, children often tend to forget that they had a 'battle' with their parents. Parents, however, often nurse those feelings of annoyance and irritation with their child for much longer periods. Similarly, a strong disagreement may have happened before the child goes to school and when he returns he behaves as if nothing had happened in the morning. That the child does not carry feelings of annoyance and irritation with his parents the rest of the day makes them think that something has to be wrong with the child. How can somebody not show any signs, or not allude to the conflict or feelings of anger, given what happened in the morning? They may not say what they think is wrong with the child, but they definitely convey that it is a sign of abnormality or 'split-personality'. This type of attribution is not uncommon with many parents. In a situation like this, the position that we have taken is that in fact it is much better that the child did not harbour those feelings all day, or even part of the day. We try to explain to parents that the reason a child does not entertain those feelings, as long as his parents do, could be a function of a number of factors, and it is not always easy to establish a reliable causative relationship. Because a child does not carry on with those feelings for a long time, it does not necessarily follow that something is pathologically wrong with the child, as a considerable number of parents under these circumstances tend to believe. In fact, it would seem to us, if anything, it is a healthy sign that the child tries to overcome his feelings of anger, resentment or negativity and returns to an even keel.

It is not always possible to form a hypothesis in each and every case as to why some parents try to attribute medical reasons as the underlying cause of their children's problems. It was however possible to form an opinion at least with one family. In that case, Mrs J wanted to prove to her mother-in-law that there was nothing wrong with the way she brought up her four-year-old son; his difficult behaviour was due to the fact that he had ADHD. We saw absolutely no evidence that this boy had any signs of ADHD. Any evidence, any views presented to Mrs J that her son did not have ADHD, were politely but firmly rejected. She set herself on a course of gaining more knowledge so that she could convince herself that her son did have ADHD. Essentially, like many other parents in this category, what this mother was trying to latch on to was some medical reasons for his behaviour difficulties rather than look at her own parenting and attributional style.

Other Types of Attributional Errors

From time to time, some parents say that with age their children's behaviours might improve even if they carried on using rewards and sanctions that they had been using unsuccessfully prior to coming to see a clinician, or without bringing about any desirable change in their interactions with their children. They seem to attribute the child's behaviour problems to his lack of maturity, which they believe is the root cause of his problems, and not the way they relate to him. Unfortunately, what such parents do not appreciate is that if they continue to reinforce wrong patterns of their behaviours, what alters with children over time is the nature of their problems. As they grow older they do not necessarily stop being difficult and demanding.

Another interesting example of an attributional error can be illustrated by briefly referring to the case of nine-year-old Bradley. When we saw Mrs H, Bradley's mother, she attributed the death of his pet rat as the key reason why he had a massive fit of temper before coming to see us, and had been, off and on, 'behaving badly'. Sometimes parents think that the cause of their children's behaviour problems is the E numbers in food or fizzy drinks. In some cases, where parents have split up, they tend to blame the other partner for their child's bad behaviour. In cases like this, one parent would assert that when their child goes to see the other parent during their access visit, on his return to his mother's house, his behaviour changes for the worse, and lasts for quite a few days. In some cases, mothers attribute their child's bad behaviour towards them as being because they are female and therefore, in their opinion, do not have the same authority and strength as their husbands.

Another sad but interesting example is that of a 13-year-old girl Layla. In the last year or so, she had twice taken an overdose. She was extremely unhappy and felt totally rejected by her mother who, she felt, had no time for her: all her mother was interested in, Layla claimed, was her new boyfriend and spending time with him. The first time they came to see us, Mrs J, Layla's mother, shouted at the top of her voice every time Layla tried to contradict what she was telling us about her. Layla accused her mother of lying about her; while Mrs J accused Layla of telling lies about *her* with the intention of presenting her as a bad mother who did not care for her daughter. Mrs J's overt hostility towards Layla was vehement in a way that is not often encountered between mother and daughter, at least in a clinic situation. Mrs J attributed Layla's difficulties to her being resentful that after years of hard life as a single parent she was having some attention and love from her boyfriend.

It is not uncommon for situations to arise where parents have divergent points of view as to the causative factors that they consider to be associated with the problem. A brief case history of 13-year-old Rachel will illustrate this. Rachel's main problem was that she reacted in quite a hostile manner if she could not have her own way. She banged doors, screamed, was rude to her parents, and sometimes attacked her father. Mrs S, her mother, attributed these behaviours to Rachel's grandparents, with whom she was exceedingly close, dying within the past two years. Her father, on the other hand, thought that she was using the death of her grandparents as an excuse. He attributed her difficult behaviour to her being a teenager who he thought – and expected – to be difficult around that age. Rachel behaved extremely well in school. Our formulation was that her parents had different ways of dealing with her behaviours. Her father tended to be more confrontational and her mother walked away when there was a conflict between Rachel and her parents. Also, if her mother said 'no' to one of Rachel's demands she would go to her father and ask him, and he often conceded to her request. It happened the other way round as well, though not as frequently.

These are some examples of the attributions parents tend to use that we have come across in our practice, in attempting to conceptualise or analyse the possible reasons, which could be the basis for their children's problem behaviours. A commonality in all these examples is that parents are making attributional errors as to the possible underlying reasons for their children's behaviours. In situations where parents fail to accept that there could be some other factors which could well be contributing to their children's problems, the situation rarely changes and parents invariably continue to have problems with their children.

Some Other Clinically Relevant Studies Pertaining to Parental Attributions

It would seem that the age of the child has some influence on parental attributions. Gretarsson and Gelfand (1988) suggest that if children are older then their parents interpret their bad behaviour and their academic difficulties more negatively, and view it as more intentional and controllable than that of younger children. Dix, Ruble, Grusec & Nixon (1986) and Slep & O'Leary (1998) suggest that when parents see children as responsible for their misbehaviours they are more likely to respond negatively to such behaviour. When they are in a negative mood, parents are more likely to attribute blame on the child for his bad behaviour. When this happens, they tend to become more punitive in their approach in dealing with children's problem behaviours (Dix 1993; Dix et al., 1990). Some studies have also observed that mothers become physically more aroused and angered by their children's unacceptable behaviours when they attribute the blame on to the child (see studies cited in Slep & O'Leary, 1998). This was clearly evident when 12-year-old Stephen's mother was describing his behaviour difficulties to us. While doing so, she became very worked up and exuded so many negative feelings towards Stephen (who was also sitting there) and what she believed he was doing to her. Not only was she attributing all the blame to him but she was not even prepared to consider that the way she dealt with him played a significant role in the way he behaved. It is little wonder that strong associations have also been found between parental attributions and psychopathology in the family (Bugental & Johnston, 2000). We have found that the way parents attribute blame is not only predictive of the quality of parent–child relationship but also of the treatment outcome.

EFFECT OF PARENTAL ATTRIBUTION ON TREATMENT PLAN

In line with our own experience, Antshel, Brewster & Waisbren (2004) state that there is a correspondence between treatment adherence and attributions parents make with regard to the underlying cause of their children's problems. Joiner and Wagner's (1996) meta-analysis of eight empirical studies provide further support to that. Reimers, Wacker,

Derby & Cooper (1995) found that when parents attributed physical causes to children's problems, they would often show resistance in accepting any psychological intervention. For instance, even when a consultant paediatrician, following all the necessary investigations, has excluded any medical basis of soiling, some parents still keep on attributing physiological reasons as the primary cause of the child's soiling and continue to show unwillingness to accept and implement psychological intervention. Furthermore, when children have a chronic health condition, parents are often less inclined to attribute blame to the child for behaviour or academic difficulties and are inclined to be less strict in disciplining them compared with the parents of healthy children (Antshel et al., 2004). In other words, there is some correspondence between the parental emotional and behavioural responses towards their children and what they believe (or attribute) to be the cause(s) of their children's problems. The grandmother, who looked after her 13-year-old granddaughter, Hayley, attributed her inability to go to school to her 'nerves'. Therefore she was very protective, emotionally supportive and was not prepared to use any undue pressure on her to go to school, despite threats from her school that if Hayley did not start attending school they would take legal action against the grandmother. Because of the way her grandmother saw the underlying cause of Hayley's problems, she feared that if she put any pressure on her, she might end up having a nervous breakdown.

If parents continue to believe in a particular reason for the child's behaviour problems despite the available contradictory evidence, and the clinician's best efforts to help them to revise their views, the chances are that, in such cases, any intervention is highly unlikely to be successful. This becomes evident when parents keep referring to it during the course of consultations, notwithstanding when alternative and possibly more plausible reasons which could be contributing to the child's difficult behaviours have been put forward to parents. For instance, Josh, an 11-year-old lad, was chiefly looked after by his retired grandparents. Josh's father lived at his parents' house, as he was divorced from his wife. He had some involvement in looking after his son when he returned from work. Josh's mother was an alcoholic and very violent. She had been imprisoned for two years for stabbing Josh's father. She blamed Josh's grandparents for the fact that he had been taken away from her, although it was in fact the social services who had decided to remove the child from her as she was deemed unfit to look after Josh. She was often abusive to Josh's grandparents and frequently destroyed their property.

Josh's mother came to see Josh quite regularly, once a week. She was not allowed to have unsupervised contact with Josh. She saw him at Josh's grandparents' house. Every week when she came, she invariably brought a little present for him. Josh's grandparents said that she often poisoned Josh's mind against them. If Josh ever complained about his grandparents to his mother, she would become very abusive and aggressive towards them. In order to avoid this happening, they often gave in to whatever reasonable or unreasonable demands Josh made. This was often because of their advanced age and the fact that they were really struggling to cope with his rather difficult behaviour. Our hypothesis as to why Josh was very difficult was simply that his grandparents invariably gave in, in order to have some peace and quiet. We regarded this as one of the major reasons why Josh ignored his grandparents and did what he wanted. On the one hand, Josh's grandparents were in full agreement with our hypothesis; on the other hand, they kept on attributing Josh's behaviour to the genes that he had inherited from his mother, because they saw many similarities between his and his mother's behaviour. Josh's grandparents always politely listened to any advice given but because of their deep down belief that the underlying cause of Josh's problems was genetic, any advice given was only half-heartedly implemented and cognitively assimilated. To this, however, it needs to be added that their age was also against them and they felt somewhat helpless and unable to cope with him or take a firm position when his demands were unreasonable. It was therefore no surprise to us that the effect of our advice was almost negligible.

If, despite the therapists' best efforts, parents continue to adhere to their 'hostile biases, blame oriented cognitions, perceived powerlessness' (Bugental & Johnston, 2000) towards the child, any success in bringing about any change in the child's behaviour is exceedingly slim. Some parents are so deeply entrenched in their views in putting all the blame on the child that we have rarely been successful in altering their attributions about the blame. (Some programmes, however, are aimed at altering parental cognitions of at-risk populations; see references cited in Bugental and Johnston, 2000.) When that does happen, according to our clinical experience, any intervention is rarely successful and it often leads to parents dropping out of the treatment plan.

It is only a small minority of parents who wonder if they must be doing 'something wrong' when their child does not behave properly; such parents often show keenness to change and improve their interactional style with their child. Before the father of 15-year-old Mickey came to see us, he described himself as extremely authoritarian and confrontational in his approach towards his son. Yet he was amazingly open and keen to adapt his interactional style with his son because he realised that his way of dealing with him was just not working. When that happens, obviously, it can influence the way parents treat their children, which can affect their future development, as well (Miller, 1995).

PARENTAL APPROACHES TO DEALING WITH CHILDREN'S PROBLEMS

When confronted with any emotional and/or behaviour problems, as one would expect, parents often first try their own strategies to deal with them, prior to seeing a CAMHS or any other professional. Approaches regularly employed by parents when their children do not behave include being cross with them, smacking, sending them to bed, withdrawal of their privileges and love, shaming and humiliating them, making them feel guilty, giving in, 'grounding' them, talking to them and so on. In a few cases, parents also say that they have used positive incentives (e.g. 'bribery', star charts) but, in their experience, either 'they do not seem to work' or if they are effective, their effect lasts only for a few days. As an example of an incentive, parents sometimes say that they have taken their child out for a meal, or for the day, and as soon as he came back, or the following day, he reverted to his oppositional or defiant behaviour again. Often with such incentives parental expectation is that once they have 'treated' their child or 'bribed' him, this should help him to sustain his good behaviour for a period of time and he should continue to display feelings of gratefulness for the favour that the parents did him. In making these observations, these parents are expressing *their* understanding as to how rewards and punishments work or do not work. We take up this issue again as in our opinion, backed by research evidence, we consider parents should use rewards and punishments – those that have true meaning to the child – as an aid to modify their behaviours.

Essentially, different parents employ different ways to discipline and control their children. In many cases their methods of dealing with their children have been greatly influenced from their own experiences of the way they were treated by their own parents. It is therefore not uncommon to hear from some parents who say that when they were children, they were given a smack when they did not behave appropriately, and this had done them no harm. The latter invariably is said in defence of their belief – and practice – that smacking children is acceptable, whether or not it helps to change their behaviour. However, we have sometimes come across parents who have gone completely the opposite way to the manner they were treated when they were little. If they received harsh treatment from their parents, when they become parents they try to be more loving, warm and affectionate towards their children compared to the way their parents were towards them. In most cases, however, before parents come to see us, their main approach of dealing with their children's problems has often been punitive.

Recently, *The Independent* (2004) reported a rather unorthodox parenting strategy adopted by two American parents of two 'ungrateful' children, aged 12 and 17. These parents felt that adopting this approach would teach these two boys how to show some appreciation for all the chores (e.g. cooking, washing their clothes, driving them to where they wished to be taken) they had normally been doing for them. The parents decided to go on 'strike' until they received co-operation and respect from them. As a part of this plan, they moved out of the house and started living in a tent that they pitched on their driveway. When the newspaper reporter interviewed them, they described their action as a 'war' between their children and themselves. They further added that, 'If we have to stick it out here until Christmas, then, ho ho, ho, we're here.' They went inside the house only to use the toilet and have a shower. They had left enough food in the freezer for the children to fend for themselves. Did this rather unconventional and theatrical approach make their children appreciate their parents' point of view? In the words of the reporter, and this couple's twelve-year-old daughter, 'There is a glimmer of hope. Kit washed her clothes for the first time. And the twelve year old appears conciliatory. "I understand why they're doing this", she admitted. "I guess we don't help out as much as we could. I am going to change"' (p. 32). According to the newspaper reporter, this novel approach did have support from other parents who drove past their house and saw what the two parents were up to.

The preceding few paragraphs might suggest that there were no major differences between the parents in their approach to dealing with their children's problems. There are, however, situations where that is not the case. Quite frequently, we see families where one parent is very punitive in his/her approach, while the other parent is far less so. In fact, sometimes, we also come across situations where one parent's way of dealing with their children is more than satisfactory and does not require any help from us, while the other parent is perhaps the main cause of the child's problems. Eight-year-old Claire presented, for a girl of her age, very serious behaviour problems at home; she literally ruled the roost in the house, and made the life of her younger sister, 18-month-old Lauren, an absolute misery. Her parents, Mr and Mrs G, argued over her and the only way they could cope with the difficulties that Claire presented was to split up: Mr G looked after the 13-year-old daughter and Mrs G looked after Claire and Lauren. Mrs G told us how she dealt with Claire and the way her husband did (incidentally, Mr G never came to see us). For instance, Mr G would give in, even when he or his wife had said no to Claire, if she persisted in her demands. Mr G's rationale for doing this was that it was easier to give in rather than be in conflict with her, which caused so much wear and tear on the whole family. Mrs G, on the other hand, set clear and firm boundaries; if she said 'no', then she meant 'no'. Equally, she was aware how to avoid unnecessary confrontation with her;

she took steps and did that. For instance, Claire was obsessed with people breathing germs on her or on her food. When Mrs G made sandwiches for lunch and if she talked at the same time, Claire would get hold of the sandwiches and throw them in the bin. To overcome this difficulty, Mrs G decided to make them when Claire had gone to bed. In other families, there can be some other types of differences between the way each parent manages their children's difficult behaviours.

Whatever disciplining approach parents have adopted, irrespective of its success or failure and irrespective of the differences, the rationale behind it all, in the vast majority of cases, has been to help their children to acquire their own and society's standards of behaviours when they are under their supervision, and when they are not.

Parenting Styles

The way parents deal with the issues related to their children's behaviour, and in general interact with them, has come to be known as parenting style. Parenting style is defined as: 'a general pattern of care giving that provides a context for specific episodes of parental childrearing behaviours; but it does not refer to a specific act or specific acts of parenting' (Wood, Mcleod, Sigman, Hwang & Chu, 2003, p. 135). In recent years, some experts have started to differentiate the terminology parenting style from parenting practices/behaviours. 'Parenting 'practices' or 'behaviours' are conceptualised as 'specific kinds of parental interactions with children in specific situations' (Wood et al., 2003, p. 135). Notwithstanding this distinction between parenting style and parenting practices/behaviours, we will use the term parenting style here for two reasons. First, the authors of the studies that we are going to refer to have used the terminology as parenting style. As it is their work that we will be referring to, therefore, it seems apposite that we use the terminology they have used. Secondly, it seems to us that their delineation of different parenting styles encompasses both the constructs parenting style and parenting practices/behaviours.

Parenting style is influenced by the temperament of the parents and the quality of their relationship with their children; it is believed to create an emotional climate for the parent–child relationship. This emotional climate can have a significant influence on the child's behaviour and personality. There is a considerable body of evidence which proposes that the absence or lack of warm and mutually rewarding relationships between children and parents can lead to emotional and behaviour problems in children. According to Deater-Deckard and Petrill (2004), 'A number of theorists have proposed that problems in the emergence of coherent, well-regulated and mutually rewarding parent–child interactions in early childhood may contribute to the development of behavioural and emotional problems in children' (2004, p. 1176). On the other hand, when the relationship is warm and caring, it can have a positive effect on children's developing self-perception, self-esteem, general mental health, as well as on positive peer relationships (Dekovic & Meeus, 1997; Hopkins & Klein, 1993; Pawlak & Klein, 1997; Xia & Qian, 2001; although we have used the word 'child', it should be noted that the actual age range of the sample included in the first study was 12–18-year-olds, and in the others were college age students). In addition to that, we have also found that, despite the interactional difficulties between children and parents, when the relationship is free from bitterness, hostility and negativity, the therapeutic outcome tends to be much more positive as opposed to when the relationship between children and parents has broken down. In addition, a nurturing atmosphere in the home can help children to have a positive view of their parents (Parish & McCluskey, 1992). We feel that it is fundamentally important that children have a positive perception of their parents and that they are not seen as 'little Hitlers', as one of our teenagers used to call his father. We won't pursue this any further here, as this point is taken up again later in this book.

Over the years, researchers working in this field have identified a number of different styles that parents use in dealing with their children and the impact that parenting style can have on children's personalities and behaviours. The most well known, and often quoted in the literature, are: authoritarian, authoritative and permissive (Baumrind, 1967, 1980). It should be noted though that these are general categories and should not be perceived as if they were discrete. It is perfectly possible to come across a parent who could employ a mixture of authoritarian and, say, permissive approaches.

Authoritarian

Parents who often use an authoritarian style are invariably strict and have fixed ideas about discipline and behaviour. A Finnish study (Aunola, Nurmi, Onatsu-Arvilommi & Pulkkinen, 1999) found that parents who use this style often have low levels of education. Such parents are inclined to use set standards to control and evaluate their children's behaviour and attitudes. These parents value obedience, respect for authority, work and tradition. Mussen, Conger, Kagan & Huston (1990) consider that some parents adopt this approach 'out of feelings of hostility or because they cannot be bothered with explanations and arguments' (p. 600), while some other parents may use this approach because they subscribe to the view that by adopting an authoritarian style they may be developing in their children respect for authority. In our experience, another reason for some parents using this style is simply because that is the only style of parenting they know (i.e. that is how they were treated by their own parents). Thirteen-year-old Dale presented, according to his mother, serious acting out problems both at home and at school. She said to us that her parents treated her in the old-fashioned way, where children were seen but not heard, whereas Dale's father treated him differently because he was one of six, and as a young lad he got away with a lot himself. As a consequence of their diverse upbringing, Dale's father tended to be laid-back in his style; she, however, was very authoritarian, which was quite evident during the initial assessment. Whenever Dale opened his mouth to say something, she would shout at him and tell him to 'shut up!'. Such an authoritarian approach can repress disagreement/disobedience but does not eradicate it. It was quite obvious in the case of Dale that his mother's authoritarian style not only failed to get his co-operation, but also caused her a lot of stress as well, as a consequence of the way she handled him.

Children of parents who routinely use an authoritarian approach tend to be moderately competent and responsible, but they also tend to be socially withdrawn and lack spontaneity. The effect of authoritarian parenting style on girls is that it is likely to create dependency on their parents and adversely affects their achievement motivation, while boys tend to become more aggressive compared to the ones who have not experienced authoritarian parenting style (Atkinson, Atkinson, Smith, Bem & Hilgard, 1990). A few studies have found some association between authoritarian parenting style and low self-esteem (Coopersmith, 1967; Pawlak & Klein, 1997). A further consequence of such an approach is that children can begin to feel resentment against their parents, when such an approach is used indiscriminately. Children who experience authoritarian upbringing are likely to perceive their parents as not loving, rejecting, unreasonable or wrong in their expectations and demands (Mussen et al., 1990, and several studies cited therein).

Authoritative

Parents who use an authoritative approach show willingness and preparedness to explain and discuss (and sometimes modify) their ideas about behaviour and discipline with their children. These parents combine a judicious mixture of 'control with acceptance and child-centred involvement'. With this type of parenting style, parents often discipline children by setting clear goals for them and take active interest in their progress. When children succeed, they often receive positive responses from their parents. Their approach to parenting shows warmth, nurturance and two-way communication. Communication between parents and children is quite an important factor which can protect children from going off the rails. The relationship between 16-year-old Charles and his mother completely broke down. When seen in the clinic situation, both mother and Charles said that their only means of communication between the two was by shouting and swearing and banging doors at each other. His mother could not cope with him and he had to go and start living with his maternal grandmother. Charles admitted to smoking 'weed' and said: 'I smoke Ganj to chill out and forget 'bout my pathetic mom [*sic*].' His behaviour in school led him to five exclusions.

Parents who use an authoritative parenting style often have a good relationship with their children. Research (see Mussen et al., 1990, and studies cited therein) shows that such parenting style tends to promote in their children independence, self-reliance, responsibility, and strong motivation to achieve. They are successful socially as well as intellectually; they tend to be popular with their peers and are often cooperative towards their parents. Parents who are accepting of their children's behaviours and feelings are likely to promote in them tolerance of negative affect which is likely to reduce their sensitivity to anxiety (Gottman, Katz & Hooven, 1997). In other words, such an approach is helpful to their children's emotional well-being.

Permissive

This approach refers to parents whose ideas about their children's behaviour and discipline are relaxed and liberal and who do not establish clear guidelines and boundaries. According to Baumrind (1991) such parents allow substantial amount of self-regulation and they tend to avoid confrontation. Often they are non-traditional, lenient and do not require mature behaviours from their children. This type of parenting style has a negative effect on their children's academic success and on their behaviours in school (Lamborn, Mounts, Steinberg & Dornbusch, 1991). As well as school-related problems, Lamborn et al. also found that these children have higher rates of substance misuse compared to children whose parents used other forms of parenting styles (e.g. authoritarian, authoritative, neglectful). A positive outcome of this type of parenting is that children raised with this type of parenting style develop higher self-esteem and better social skills.

In addition to the foregoing brief description of diverse parenting styles, in recent years, some researchers in this field have identified some other parental styles as well. This includes autonomy, intrusiveness, emotional over-involvement, inconsistency, and disturbances in communication styles. These various parenting styles are less likely to be known to many professionals in the field compared to those described above. However, these various parenting styles do not necessarily encompass 'all forms of parenting behaviour across the normal and pathological range' (O'Connor, 2002, p. 556). What this shows is that there is a whole range of different approaches that parents adopt with their children when they deal with them, under normal circumstances, and when they have to discipline them because they are not happy with their behaviours. As one would expect, it is highly likely that many parents would use different parenting styles at different times and under different circumstances. Furthermore, sometimes, parents may be more permissive when children are younger, and stricter when they are older; likewise, there can be differences between the ways boys and girls are treated; the way the first-born and later born children are treated (we have considered this topic at some length on p. 40). In addition to all this, it is not uncommon for mothers and fathers to have a different parenting style (Atkinson et al., 1990). Perhaps what is important is that different types of parenting style are likely to have different types of impact on children's behaviours and personality (see O'Connor, 2002, and some of the studies cited therein).

Irrespective of the different parenting styles, the child, however, should not be regarded as a passive recipient of parenting style. Temperament and behaviour of children influence the responses they evoke from others. Fifteen-year-old Ryan said to us that his ten-year-old brother got more attention, love, and financial rewards from his parents because he was more agreeable at home than him, although, outside the house, he behaved just as deviantly (e.g. shoplifting, smoking, drinking, fighting) as Ryan did.

Notwithstanding the diverse mixture of parenting styles, we have noticed one common thread in a vast majority of parents of all classes that we have seen in clinics, in schools or during home visits. That is, irrespective of socio-economic background, a very high percentage of the parents want to do their best for their children – perhaps with the exception of parents who physically and emotionally abuse them. While the vast majority of parents have the best intentions for their children, their parenting style is not always conducive to producing good behaviours in them. It does not mean that everything they do is wrong. We are sure that there are lots of things that they do with their children that are right, although they may not be fully aware of them, or may not see it that way: obviously, it is the clinicians' responsibility to highlight and reinforce that. Were clinicians to do that, it would help parents to feel more positively about themselves; because often many parents of children with behaviour problems have a very low opinion about their parenting skills

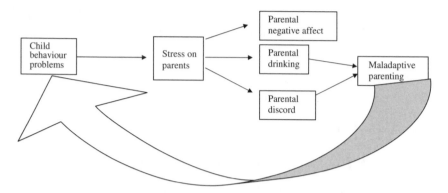

Figure 2.2 Schematic representation of the relationship between parental stress and children's behaviour problems (adapted from Pelham & Lang, 1999)

and feel responsible for their children's behavioural difficulties; and that makes them feel guilty and downhearted. They reason to themselves, rightly or wrongly, that if they were not the cause of their children's difficulties, they would not be having any problems with them. The other obvious benefit is that because they have been endorsed and positively reinforced by the clinician, this is likely to encourage parents to use those strategies more frequently compared to what they had done in the past. Obviously, all this should have a helpful effect on the way they manage their children and on the family dynamics.

Unfortunately, there are also many factors that influence the way many parents deal with their children that leads to conflict between them and which in turn causes them (both parents and children) a lot of unhappiness, feelings of guilt as well as stress. When parents are stressed, they often become irritable, more punitive, more demanding, perhaps more authoritarian, and have unrealistic expectations compared with when they are not so stressed. In short, it impairs their parenting style. When that happens, this makes children more difficult and they react badly to that type of parenting behaviour. It creates a kind of vicious cycle (see also Bugental & Johnson, 2000) which is sometimes difficult to break. This can be represented schematically as shown in Figure 2.2.

It is therefore absolutely critical that such a vicious cycle is broken. This is where the skilled role of a clinician and of books like this comes in. In saying this, however, it is imperative to add that it is not implied that *all* families benefit either with our approach or with the approaches adopted by other experts. Some of the reasons for this have been alluded to in this book where it has been considered appropriate and necessary. This is not just our experience but that of other workers in this field as well (Hartman et al., 2003).

3

CLINICAL CONCERNS, RAISED BY PARENTS, WHICH HAVE THEORETICAL UNDERPINNINGS

The major focus of this chapter is to address some of the issues which parents have repeatedly raised with us during our consultations with them. We have tried to deal with those topics here both at a practical level and, where possible, supported our stance with selected research. Given the slant of the book (i.e. to be of practical use to recently qualified CAMHS clinicians or to those who are in training), we did not feel that we needed to refer to the relevant literature comprehensively while dealing with these issues: hence the references are somewhat selective.

We regard the topics discussed in this chapter as being of considerable importance; hence we have devoted a whole chapter to addressing them. The reason for this is because they challenge parents' belief systems. For instance, a parent, prior to coming and seeing a clinician, may not believe or appreciate how the environment and genes interact, or the importance of environment on the child's behaviour. Frequently, they come believing resolutely that it is just genes which determine our behaviour. If parents continue to hold on to this belief, they are unlikely to accept the role of the environment on our behaviours and the interaction between genes and the environment. This in turn has implications for them in changing the way they interact with their children. Unless they can be convinced of that, they may not be prepared to change the way they view their children's behaviours. In other words, their continued belief in some of the areas that we outline below can influence the therapeutic outcome. It therefore needs to be explained very carefully to parents about the inter-action between genes and environment and how the latter can have a profound effect on the way we all behave. We will even go to the extent of saying that, where possible, parents need to be convinced of this, although it may not always be likely.

DIFFICULTIES IN ESTABLISHING CAUSE AND EFFECT RELATIONSHIP WITH BEHAVIOUR

Sometimes it is not difficult to see why a child is behaving badly in a specific situation. This could simply be because a child may not want to wear a particular dress or want to eat a particular food. In situations like this, one can speculate with reasonable certainty that not being allowed to wear the child's preferred clothing, or not given the food the child wants is the cause of the problem. More often than not it is not that easy to establish exactly the underlying reason or reasons for the child's bad behaviour. Notwithstanding that, even in very complex family circum- stances, parents sometimes think that they know exactly why their child misbehaves. Some of the examples that parents have used include: he is all right so long as he can get what he wants or can have his own way; he is violent like his father; two members in the family have schizophre- nia so he must be schizophrenic and that is why his behaviour is perfectly satisfactory in school but he is absolutely awful at home, which just shows that he has a 'split personality'.

In cases where parents do not have a firm view of the underlying reason for the child's undesirable behaviour, they often then expect that the clini- cian should be able to explain the accurate cause of their child's deviant behaviour. Consider the following two examples.

When Mark's mother (Mrs S) was pregnant with him, his parents lost their seven-year-old son. The effect was so devastating on Mrs S that she did not wish to go through this experience again. So when she had Mark, she decided not to love him and felt very cold towards him. She also said that her own parents used to be very cold towards her when she was a little girl. In addition, she suffered from post-natal depression. Mark's father, Mr S, therefore had to carry out his early upbringing. He literally did everything for him. It was from the age of two onwards that Mrs S started to show some interest in him. When they came to see us, Mark was about twelve years old. Among other problems, there are two that are relevant here. First, Mark followed his father around and, as he put it, he 'could not have a break from him', which Mr S found very stifling. When he went to have a bath, Mark would knock at his door and ask if he was OK. When he returned from school, if he could not see his father, the first thing that he would ask his mother would be where his father was. On the other hand, he never asked for his mother. Secondly, notwith- standing Mark's being so attached to his father, he said very hurtful things to him. Mark would say to his father that he wished that when he went out, a car would drive over him and kill him. To hurt Mr S even further, he sometimes also said that he was not his biological father. For Mr S, it was very puzzling that, on the one hand, Mark followed him around and, on the other hand, Mark said very upsetting things to him. Mr S wanted to know *precisely* what made Mark say such unkind things to him.

In our second example, the mother of a twelve-year-old girl, a single parent, lived in a reconstituted large family, and wanted to know the exact reason why her daughter's behaviour at school was acceptable but at home she was totally out of control.

When parents have asked us to establish cause–effect relationships, our position invariably has been that with behaviour it is virtually impossible to establish a simple causative relationship. The reason for this is that for a long time so many factors are – and have been – impinging on our behaviours. In addition to all the unknown factors, there could be ongoing factors such as underprivileged housing, mental illness, reconstituted family situation, lack of family involvement, family dysfunction, influence of peers, influence of school, the awful experience of the way the parents were brought up by their own parents, the child's and parents' own early history and so on. All these factors interact and can be further compounded by the way we think, feel and construe things (cf. Rutter, 1980; see also Figure 2.1, p. 7).

In view of this, we, therefore, do not think that it is really possible to pinpoint one or two factors and be able to say with any certainty that such and such factors must be the underlying reason(s) for the way the child behaves. Our general view is that this applies not only to children who are referred to clinics up and down the country but to all of us. It may be easier with some of the sciences to establish an almost perfect relationship. For instance, if one puts litmus paper in some solution and it turns red, it can be said with near certainty that the acid in the solution must have caused it. In a condition like this, one can with some confidence establish a cause and effect relationship. With behaviours, on the other hand, at best, one can say that some of the factors that have been identified may have made some contribution to the child's problems. To what extent they are responsible or have contributed, one can only guess. The following poignant and true story of Kevin adds further support to our point of view as expressed here.

Kevin was one of six children and grew up on a council estate in Croydon, South London. His mother was of limited intellectual ability and was hospitalised under section 6 of the Mental Health Act. His father was an engineer. When Denis, Kevin's father, got home from work, he would normally shut himself away with a bottle of gin and Elvis Presley recordings. The house he grew up in had the smell of urine everywhere (as described in the social worker's report). Kevin was regularly attacked with fists, belts, broomsticks; on one occasion, he had his fingers fed into a wringer. After one of his mother's attacks, Kevin counted 20 bite marks on his neck, shoulders and arms where she had bitten him with her gums, using all her strength. Kevin in his book, *The Kid*, adds: 'If she had had her teeth in she would have ripped my throat out with the power of those bites' (Lewis, 2003, p. 105). There were times with his father when Kevin would be lucky to get away with his life. Despite all his best efforts to make things work out, his life spiralled out of control. At the age of 17, not able to make a proper living, he became caught up in the criminal underworld of London.

Although experiencing such a violent and awful childhood, not only has Kevin managed to survive, but he now seems to be prospering and well-established. Could anybody, with any *conviction*, identify what factor(s) could be responsible for helping Kevin, despite his circumstances, to not turn out like his parents? Our answer is no; people may speculate and make general statements about 'protective factors' (see Buchanan, Flouri & Ten Brinke, 2002, for a discussion of protective factors; Burt, Hay, Pawlby, Harold & Sharp, 2004, state that children's cognitive ability and supportive family environments can act as protective factors) that could have helped him to cope with his dreadful circumstances, but cannot establish a causative relationship.

It is therefore absolutely imperative that parents are helped to appreciate the impossibility of establishing a perfect causative relationship and that the reasons underlying a particular behaviour could be complex and stem from a number of factors. If, however, parents continue to hold on to their belief system about the reason for the child's bad behaviour, which may not be quite commensurate with the position that we have outlined here, it is highly likely that the intervention offered may not be successful. Obviously, some parents are likely to accept the clinician's explanation, while some would continue to hang on to their own views.

BI-DIRECTIONALITY

Unlike many CAMHS professionals, when we send our first appointment letter to parents, we invariably suggest they should not bring their child with them for their first one or two sessions with us. In one case, as soon as the parents walked into the interview room, the first thing they said was: 'Why didn't you want to see the child and only them? It's the child who has the problems, not us.' What this questioning of the parents shows is the way they see the child's difficulties. There is a clear suggestion in their questioning that the child's problems are child based and their interactions with the child play no part in them. Although a considerable number of parents we see may not question us as to why in our initial assessment we are only seeing them and not the child, they are often still inclined to think that the sole reason for the child's unacceptable behaviour lies with the child.

Perhaps a very familiar example to many clinicians of such a situation would be where the child's behaviour is described as perfectly satisfactory at school, or when he is with his grandparents, or with a particular aunt or an uncle, but at home he is absolutely appalling. When the parents are asked how it is that a child can behave so well in such situations but not at home, many fail to see that there must be something in their interactions, which could be an important factor in making the child behave the way he does at home. A vast majority fail to see their contribution to the child's behaviour problems, but continue to blame the child for his bad behaviour. An interesting example of such a situation was when the parents of an eight-year-old boy, Jason, was seen by one of our colleagues. Jason behaved extremely well in almost all situations except when he was with his parents at home. Even after 11 months of therapeutic input from our colleague, his parents continued to believe that something was psychiatrically wrong with their child and that he needed to see a psychiatrist. Additionally, these parents complained about a clinical psychiatric nurse who had made these parents feel that they needed to change their parenting style when they resolutely believed that nothing was wrong with the way they managed the child; it was the child who required his 'head looking at by a psychiatrist'!

In cases like this, that parents' perception of the problem ignores what the developmental psychologists describe as the bi-directionality principle. Put very simply, as with any relationship, the behaviour of one influences the behaviour of the other. What this means is that there is an interaction between the child's temperament and attributes and the parental responses to it. The way parents deal with children influences their behaviour; the way children behave influences parents' behaviour towards them. This process begins to happen even when the child is very young. A considerable body of research has shown that there is a close correspondence between aggressive children and parental physical punishment. This concomitance would suggest that either children learn to act aggressively from their parents or that parents respond by being physically punitive to their children's aggressive behaviours (e.g. Bell, 1979). Another example is where mothers of young children frequently spend time on joint activities with their children, which can have an inhibiting effect on the children developing behaviour problems. On the other hand, children who are difficult may discourage parents from spending time with them on joint activities (Galboda-Liyanage, Prince & Scott, 2003).

It is often hard to say which person was originally the most responsible for certain interactional patterns. However, some researchers in this field think that it may be possible in certain situations to infer who influences whose behaviour (Campbell, 1979; Chess et al., 1965; see also Thomas, Chess & Birch, 1968). This may be the case with some babies who are very demanding; they seem to influence the reactions they receive from their mothers. As an example, babies who are very difficult to manage (with irregular patterns of eating, sleeping and bowel movement; who cry a lot and show mostly negative moods, are irritable and do not adjust to changes easily) often deprive mothers of the satisfaction and pleasure of having a baby, feelings they anticipated before the birth. Such infants are likely to be very frustrating to their mothers and often elicit hostile reactions from them; such reactions, in turn, tend to increase the infant's irritability and make them even more difficult. Temperamental difficulties such as these can invariably result in an unsatisfactory mother–infant relationship and may lead to a cycle of unhelpful interactions between the baby and his mother; in a case such as this, a problem started by the baby's behaviour and the mother's reaction to it. Another point, however, could be that pre-natal stress, health, etc., could have influenced the baby's development *in utero* and contributed to his temperament.

Yet another such example could be of young children who are overly active, lack self-control, are oppositional and do not often comply with their parents' instructions. Mothers of such children are often more controlling, give more commands and are more critical than mothers of typical children. Some of these parental behaviours may be at first influenced by their children's overactivity; the children's behaviour in turn is influenced by their mothers' reactions to them (Mash & Johnston, 1982).

Apart from the preceding scenarios, on the whole parents' influence is likely to be greater in shaping their children's behaviour than the other way round. Parental influence has an effect not only on their children's overt behaviour but also on the way they start internalising standards and expectations, which they have imbibed as a result of their interactions with their parents (see Deater-Deckard & Bullock, 2003, and several studies cited therein). Having internalised these behaviours, children then often generalise them in other situations and relationships (Grusec & Kuczynski, 1977).

IS BEHAVIOUR STABLE OVER TIME?

If a child throws up temper tantrums at two, is he going to be difficult when he is adolescent?

For understandable reasons, some parents often express concern and ask us if their children will grow out of their externalising or other unacceptable behaviours. What they are asking clinicians to do is to predict their children's behaviour from the way they behave now. What some research shows (e.g. Tremblay et al., 1999) is that many children who exhibit aggression around two years old manage to control it by the time they are about to start school. However, some research (Olson, Bates, Sandy & Schilling, 2002, and several studies cited therein; Tremblay, Masse, Vitaro & Dobkin, 1995; see also Huesmann, Eron & Dubow, 2002; Kingston & Prior, 1995; Seguin, Arseneault, Boulerice, Harden & Tremblay, 2000; Vitaro, Tremblay, Gagnon & Boivin, 1992) suggests that children who show disruptive behaviours when they are of kindergarten age are likely to manifest far more serious problems (e.g. delinquency, school failure, substance misuse) later. Burt, Hay, Pawlby, Harold & Sharp (2004), in their longitudinal study, also found that in one of their sub-groups, intellectual difficulties at four years of age were linked with disruptive behaviour at age 11. In their second subgroup, they found that in situations where mothers and children showed psychological problems when the child was four years of age, the children were disruptive when they were 11. Some studies also show that young children who are not good at delaying immediate gratification, who have difficulty in inhibiting impulsive behaviour, and who do not respond to task situations in a planned manner, are at risk of developing a range of behavioural, social and academic difficulties during childhood and adolescence (Calkins, 1994; Campbell et al., 2000). Some researchers (as cited in Juffer, Bakermans-Kranenburg & Jzendoorn, 2005) have shown that disorganised attachment during infancy is predictive of later problems in managing stress, externalising behaviour problems, and dissociated behaviour in adolescence.

Despite the availability of research evidence which points to the fact that if children display certain types of behaviours when they are very young that forebodes serious problem behaviours later, we are, in the main, very cautious – and reluctant – to make any firm predictions about children's future behaviour on the basis of their present behaviour, for the following reasons.

1. We agree with Kazdin (2003) when he says, 'many risk factors have no causal role in the onset or maintenance of a problem' (p. 81). It would also seem that the studies which advocate that predictions about how the child is likely to behave in future have only modest correlations: 'predictive associations have been modest and with the exception of the Caspi group, prior studies have been based solely on maternal reports of infant/toddler temperament' (Olson et al., 2002, p. 436).
2. Herbert (1994) cautions that many studies which have made predictions are unsound on methodological grounds. By referring to a study by Yarrow et al. (1968), Herbert explains that in many of those researches

'follow-back designs' have been used and 'they can be somewhat unreliable in their inferences; which limit the conclusions researches can safely make' (p. 104).

3. Things change as children grow older; they have a whole range of experiences: what kind of impact those changes and experiences are going to have and how they are going to shape their future behaviour, we simply do not know. For instance, there is some evidence (Caspi & Roberts, 1999; Goldsmith et al., 1987: both studies cited in Cote, Tremblay, Nagin, Zoccolillo & Vitaro, 2002, p. 615) which suggests that the 'social context' of the child can alter the child's personality traits. It is not infrequent for clinicians to come across cases where a child at home behaves perfectly satisfactorily and is extremely difficult in school or vice versa. Another interesting, but uncommon example is that of a ten-year-old boy, Leroy, whose parents were of West Indian origin. Leroy's main problems were oppositional behaviour and some stealing. His parents felt very angry with Leroy that he invariably destroyed his toys. The way he behaved at home caused a lot of stress for them, particularly his mother who said that she had suffered from depression as a result of it. The family had a close friend, Molly, who lived by herself. In order to give Leroy's mother a break, she became quite involved in looking after him. Leroy would go and stay with Molly at weekends or during the school holidays. When he was at 'Aunty Molly's' house, Leroy's behaviour was perfectly acceptable. We asked 'Aunty Molly' whether given the way Leroy behaved at her house, she would feel the need to seek advice from an agency such as ours. Her answer was a firm 'no'. We appreciate that the example of Leroy is not purely of change in the 'social context' but also the way he was treated by 'Aunty Molly'.

4. If a clinician tells a parent that because their child at the age of three or four is disruptive he is likely to be delinquent, or do badly at school when he is older, what impact will it have on the parents, and on their efforts to modify the child's behaviour? We assume it would be devastating, it would adversely effect their expectations, and may even have an undesirable effect on their attempts to do something about the child's current bad behaviour. This is particularly true when evidence seems to suggest that intervention at an earlier stage of disruptive behaviours can be more effective than its manifestation at a later stage (Denham et al., 2002). Likewise, right intervention at the right stage can also lower the rate of disorganised attachment and thereby reduce the problems that may manifest at a later stage (Juffer, Bakermans-Kranenburg & Jzendoorn, 2005).

5. There are also questions of generalisability about some of the behavioural characteristics, which have been found to be stable over a period

of time. For instance, Cote et al. (2002) found considerable similarity on the measures of fearfulness and helpfulness when first measured at kindergarten level and then when the children finished primary school. In spite of substantial stability in these measures from the age of six through to 12, the authors rightly caution: 'we cannot exclude that part of the stability may reflect consistency within a specific context (i.e. school) and not necessarily consistency across contexts' (p. 615).

6. The issue of stability over time is not that simple. One of the reasons for this is that some behaviours are more stable than others and some periods of development are more stable than others. According to Michel (1968 cited in Mussen et al., 1990), altruism and helpfulness are not quite stable over time; individuals can change with age and possibly with different experiences. There is some further recent evidence, based on an Australian longitudinal study, which demonstrates that 11–12-year-old 'high-risk' children when followed till the age of 18, only a quarter of them developed consistent patterns of anti-social behaviour despite these children going through a difficult phase of puberty. When these children were selected for this longitudinal study (the total sample consisted of 10,000 children) some of the behaviours which they displayed included being volatile, uncooperative, having poor self-control, having short attention span, and being hyperactive. At least three of these factors had to be present to be included in this study. The fact that three-quarters of these children displayed high-risk behaviours when they were around 11–12, and yet still managed to thrive, was attributed to strong parenting and good schooling (reported in *The Observer* by Martin Bright, 2004).

7. From early childhood onwards, our life experiences and our interactions with them continue to shape our personality and behaviours (Atkinson et al., 1990). This can be illustrated by two case studies. Daniel was an 11-year-old boy who lived with his mother because his parents were divorced. He had two elder sisters and a brother. His elder brother had some behavioural problems when he was young. Up until junior school, Daniel's overall behaviour was age-appropriate and during his junior school phase, he never refused to go to school. However, after the first few weeks of starting secondary school, he stopped going to school. He started to display behaviour problems, which he had never done before. His mother had to involve the police as he was spotted wandering about in the local town with another boy and also travelling around on different buses. A week before his mother went to see her family doctor, she told him that Daniel had locked himself in his room, was throwing things out of the window and had set fire to his bedroom curtains. He had also become very bitter and frequently started to swear at the members of his family. These changes

in his behaviours took place following some experiences in the secondary school and which could not have been predicted earlier.

8. The second example is that of Charles. Some aspects of this case have been mentioned elsewhere in this book. Essentially, this boy felt neglected and rejected by his mother, who was divorced and was living with her boyfriend. Charles mixed with the wrong type of peer group, had several police warnings, and was permanently excluded from school. During the previous consultation, he was convinced in his mind that smoking 'weed', getting drunk at weekends, going without food at weekends and using that food money to buy alcohol and drugs, were all perfectly acceptable. If an adult disagreed with that, they were not in their right mind! He flew off the handle if things did not go his way. During this session, he was asked to think what effect the regular use of drugs and excessive alcohol could be having on his physical and mental development since he was still growing. The next appointment following this was six weeks later and during the intervening period Charles had found himself a girlfriend. When he was seen at this time, his mother, who had previously been unable to accept anybody praising him, and certainly would not say anything nice to him herself, said unreservedly that he was a changed boy. Not only had he stopped abusing drugs and alcohol, there had been a major shift in his views about them. He realised that they were bad for him and was taking active steps to stop using them completely. In addition, he had also started weight training and eating sensibly. He had been much more respectful to his mother in comparison with his previous behaviour. He was followed up for the next nine months and had managed to sustain this improvement. Mum and Charles attributed this significant change to his girlfriend and coming to see us. Before we started seeing him and his family, we could never have predicted such a dramatic change in Charles.

9. It is not uncommon to come across individual cases that defy all predictions. The case of Jane Tomlinson is one such example, as reported in the *Independent on Sunday* on 6 June 2004. When Jane Tomlinson was 26 years old, she was diagnosed with breast cancer. In 2000, doctors also found that she had secondary metastatic bone cancer and it was predicted that she had only six months to live. When this case was reported in the *IoS*, Jane Tomlinson was 40 years old. We are sure that Jane Tomlinson's is not the only case where the original prognosis turned out to be wrong; there are likely to be many more.

Because of these considerations, the position that we take when we are asked to predict is to convey to parents that it is very difficult to forecast reliably about the child's future behaviour at a very young age, despite the availability of some research evidence to which we have alluded above. Our views on this matter are quite neatly summed up by Professor Jay Belsky: 'despite all the recent research there is still no formula for predicting how a young child [during his course of development] will respond to a set of circumstances' (Professor Jay Belsky,[1] cited in *The Sunday Times*, 7 September 2003, pp. 4 and 9). We wholly share this view and share it with parents when we are asked to make any predictions about their children.

Given the unreliability of predictions, clinicians therefore need to exercise great caution in predicting future behaviours based on the current evidence. What is important is to engage and offer parents intervention programmes which help children change their behaviours (e.g. as described in this book). However, we must add that we are not claiming here that ours is the only effective approach that is useful in modifying children's behaviours and indirectly contributes to the improvement in the family functioning.

NATURE VERSUS NURTURE

Theoretical issues of *nature versus nurture* are not just the domain of, and a topic of debate amongst, theologians, philosophers and scientists. This topic is often also raised by parents in a clinical situation, who are concerned about their children's behaviour. Questions of this nature invariably come up where a parent wonders whether their child's problems are genetically determined. Problems related to the issue of nature versus nurture crop up with single or divorced mothers whose husbands or partners have been violent, abusive and/or aggressive towards their wives. When they see their children behaving in a more or less similar manner, they then tend to assume that their behaviour must be genetically determined. (However, we should also add that *this does not mean that this subject is exclusively queried by such parents only; this can be raised by other parents as well.*) For instance, 11-year-old Kirsty's mother wondered if her aggressive and violent behaviour was due to her genes because her father used to be aggressive towards her (i.e. Kirsty's mother). Seven-year-old Omar's mother said that when her son was angry and violent, he looked very much like his father, who was also violent; this violence was the cause of divorce between the parents. Omar's mother firmly believed that genetic factors were the key reason for his bad behaviour, despite the fact that at school he was described as an extremely well-behaved boy. As further confirmation that there were close similarities between her ex-husband and Omar, his mother reported that his father too could behave well and be a very nice person. In view of these likenesses between Omar and his father, she felt quite strongly that Omar's behaviour must be genetically determined.

Eleven-year-old Mark presented a number of problems. He lived in a very deprived and run-down area where young children showed little respect for other people's property: some of them even threw bricks at Mark's windows. One of Mark's problems was that he flew off the handle very easily, apparently without any reason. When he was very angry, he threw things and also destroyed them. He said that he was unable to control himself if people said things about his mother. So when his mother came to see us and had described his behaviour, she wondered if Mark might have a split personality because one minute he could be nice and the next minute he could be a 'monster'. Her additional reason for thinking that Mark could be suffering from schizophrenia was because they had one or two members in the family who had this condition, and concluded that he could have inherited those genes from the other family members.

When we are asked our opinion whether a particular behaviour or behaviours could be due to the genes that their children have inherited from parents or close family members, we take the following two-pronged position:

1. as described above: with behaviour it is not simple to establish a causative relationship;
2. in line with current thinking, we take the interactionist view: genes and experience interact with each other and help shape our personality and childhood behaviour disorders (see also Morrell & Murray, 2003). The following quotation sums up our views on this matter:

> [A] great deal of research, particularly recently, has emphasised that most of the fundamental processes of brain development are sensitive to non-genetic influences and, in particular, to experience. Forms of cellular plasticity not anticipated a decade ago are now widely accepted and have been demonstrated to be responsive to experience, including astrocytic interactions with neurons, myelination, the formation of new blood vessels, and the formation of new neurons. (Grossman, Churchill, McKinney, Kodish & Otte, 2003, p. 54; see also Emde & Hewitt, 2001, cited in Shiner & Caspi, 2003)

Ridley (2003) also expresses a similar point of view when he says that there is a circular relationship between genes and the environment. Genes are switched on and off throughout our lives depending what they come across in our surroundings; this process enables our brains and bodies to adapt to the environment. Basing his argument on numerous examples of both human and animal behaviour, Ridley advances the view that our environment affects the way our genes express themselves. He believes that humans have genetic 'thermostats' and factors in the environment have the potential to turn them up and down.

Not only do we subscribe to the view that there is an interaction between genes and environment, we also think that it is impossible to determine how much genes have contributed and how much experiences have contributed to a particular behaviour. How genes and environment interact is well explained by a distinguished Canadian psychologist, Donald Hebb, by using a simple analogy of a rectangle: it is as apposite today, as it was three decades ago. Hebb (1972) said that from an area of a rectangle, we cannot infer how much length has contributed and how much width has contributed to the area; likewise, when it comes to behaviour (including intelligence) we cannot exactly say how much it is due to our genetic make up and how much it is due to our experiences. Kagan (1997) has explained the same idea of interaction somewhat differently by using a different metaphor: 'The personality of an adult is a grey cloth made up of very thin white fibres representing biology and very thin black fibres representing experience, so intricately interwoven that the black fibres cannot be discerned from the white. All one sees is grey' (p. 149). With regard to experience, it is also important to remember that, as we are now living in a multicultural society, our experiences are shaped by the specific culture, social group and family experiences in which we have grown up (Atkinson et al., 1990). In other words, the experiences of an Asian child growing up in an Asian household in this country would be different from a child who has grown up in a 'white middle class' home (see Gupta, 1983; Gupta & Coxhead, 1990).

In the brief vignettes of Kirsty, Omar and Mark that we have outlined above, we cannot say whether their behaviour is entirely genetically based or is due to the influence of environmental factors alone. Nor can one say even in far more serious cases such as Jeffrey Dahmer, a serial killer, who, in a most gruesome manner, murdered 16 young men and was given 16 life sentences by a US court in 1992. Each of these young men was enticed to Dahmer's apartment, where Dahmer drugged and strangled them. Dahmer exposed their internal organs, and carried out various fetishistic behaviours before he dismembered their bodies; in certain cases, he even ate one or the other organs. When he had disposed of the remains, he kept some parts as mementoes. In his apartment, police found several spray-painted skulls on a coffee table, three torsos in various stages of dismemberment, several containers of body parts, and human organs in the fridge. Graham (2000) looked at the further details of this horrific case and came to the conclusion:

Dahmer has a 'normal' younger brother reared in the same home environment by the same biological parents. If Dahmer's pathology has a genetic basis or was the product of upbringing, his brother might be expected to show some signs of disturbance. On this basis, therefore, it does not seem possible to resolve the issue one way or another. Indeed, Dahmer's biographical details could be used to argue for an interactionist perspective – the idea that nature and nurture combined to influence the course of his development. (pp. 280–1)

Thus, the interaction between nature and nurture, as well as shaping the personalities and behaviours of extreme cases like that of Dahmer, are also instrumental in influencing the vast majority of the general population.

BIRTH ORDER AND PSYCHOLOGICAL TRAITS

When there is more than one child in the family, and one of them presents behaviour problems, parents often say that they brought up all of them in the same way, that they love them all the same, and are confused at how the referred child presented problems and behaved so differently from his other siblings. Often, in fact, at times they also think that the referred child ends up getting more attention, more material goods compared to his other siblings who behave within the acceptable limits. It is particularly puzzling for many parents when their other children, as they see it, are well behaved. Parents claim that the other children in the family do as they are told; they do not throw temper tantrums or sulk and so on, like the referred child. Parents invariably reject their children's observations about their parenting style which may suggest that they prefer their other siblings or treat them better than the problem child. Almost all the parents find it hard to understand.

Often, in what parents say about the referred child, there is invariably an implicit implication that something is inherently wrong with *him*. If something were not wrong with him, he would not misbehave when the behaviour of his other siblings is perfectly satisfactory, particularly when he has been treated the same way as his other siblings. This reasoning is used to convey that their management of the child's behaviour is satisfactory. While parents' bewilderment and logic about this is understandable, however, their implication, in a vast majority of the cases, that something must be wrong with the child is not correct.

In raising this concern, what parents are conveying is their lack of appreciation and understanding of the effect that birth order has on children's personality and behaviour. There could be a number of reasons why the ordinal position has an important bearing on the child's behaviour and personality and why they are all different from each other. Each reason, singly and cumulatively, has some bearing on the child's personality and behaviour. Outlined below are some of the reasons as to why the ordinal position influences the child's behaviour and personality:

1. With the first child, parents have no experience of bringing up children. Perhaps there is more trial and error with the first one, as opposed to the second and the subsequent children. Often parents think and say – rightly or wrongly – that they made some mistakes with the first child, which they did not repeat with the succeeding children.
2. If it is not completely an unwanted child, the first-born child has more time alone with parents than the subsequent children. Because of this, parents are able to do more things with him than with the second or third child.
3. Eisenman (1992) found that with the first-born child, parents tended to be more restrictive than with the later born children. This seems to be particularly true in the case of girls, as parents tend to be more protective of girls than boys.
4. Lewis & Jaskir (1983) studied the effect of the birth of the second sibling on the interaction between the first-born children and their mothers. The observation of this interaction took place in a playroom setting, first when they were 12 months old – they had no sibling then – and the second observation, when they were 24 months old. The group, who had acquired a sibling in the intervening period, displayed the following differences in their mother's interaction with them compared to when they were first observed when they were 12 months old. The relationship between the mother and the child became less playful and more strained following the birth of a second child. Lewis and Jaskir noted some changes in the behaviour of children as well. On the whole, they started to demonstrate more dependency behaviour towards their mothers and were more upset during their free play session compared to children who had not had a sibling during this 12-month period. Lewis and Jaskir further add that these changes were observed not only in the laboratory setting but at home as well.
5. A study by Abrams & Coie (1981) found that mothers of first-born boys were more likely to seek outside professional help for problems compared to mothers of later-born boys.
6. Birth order and family size can have an effect on children's achievement (Sputa and Paulson, 1995). Eisenman (1992) thinks that because first-born children have a lot more adult input than the children born subsequently, they therefore tend to achieve more than the later-born children.
7. In our clinical work, we have frequently experienced that parents unwittingly start making unrealistic demands from the oldest child

in the family which are not commensurate with his age, ability, and emotional development (cf. Chess & Thomas, 1999). They often expect him to behave in a much older way than the child actually is (we have described this as unrealistic expectations, and it has been treated at length elsewhere in this book and therefore we won't restate our views on this matter here). Suffice it to say, when that happens, it invariably leads to the child feeling resentment against their parents and to feelings of not being treated fairly. When children entertain such feelings against their parents, obviously, this can have a significant adverse effect on the whole family dynamics and children's behaviour in general and how they feel towards the other siblings in the family.

8. Sputa & Paulson (1995) found that ninth-grade students felt that the ordinal position and family size had an effect on their parents' parenting style and on their parents' involvement with them – but that was not the perception of the parents. Parents did not think that the family size and the birth order had any impact on the way they treated their children. The following three vignettes of three grown-up women aged 43 (eldest daughter), 42 (middle daughter) and 40 (youngest daughter) of their own perception of how they were treated differently by their parents because of their birth order provide further support to the points that have been made above.

Siobhan, 43, eldest daughter

Siobhan felt that her parents had high expectations of all of them, but as the oldest, she was given the biggest part of the dreams and ambitions they harboured for the whole family. Her father wanted a son and she became the honorary boy: she was the one expected to shine at sport and had to fight to protect her sisters. She was expected to be the warrior. They always thought that she was the cleverest, the one who would go to the best university and achieve most in life. But while that meant she felt special from an early age, as she got older the pressure got too much and she rebelled. She felt her true nature had been obscured under the mass of her parents' expectations and she went on the dole.

To some degree, Siobhan always envied the positions of her sisters in the family. As the middle one who perhaps escaped some of her parents' attention and had a lot more freedom than Siobhan ever experienced, Maire [the second daughter] developed a fantastic ability to socialise which Siobhan does not have.

As the youngest, Niamh managed to escape her parents' close attention and had a lot more freedom than Siobhan had ever experienced. On the other hand, she suspected Niamh might have felt a bit crushed and over-whelmed by having two older sisters who seized the attention, so her position was not easiest.

Maire, 42, middle daughter

Maire's personality was influenced by her position in the family, but she felt that being the middle child was fantastic and that it was the best position in which one could possibly be when there were three children in the family:

> Siobhan was the first-born and was very much wanted, and my parents were delighted for her. I came along a year later and I think the thrill had worn off a bit by then. But although I never felt like I was as cherished as Siobhan was as a baby, I kind of accepted her place as the special first-born without feeling resentful of it. By being in the middle of the family, I evaded the major expectations of my parents and was allowed to discover who I really was at my own pace. I was not pigeonholed like the other two . . . I am definitely more outgoing than my sisters. The role I felt was presented to me as the middle child was to be the diplomat acting as bridge and peacemaker between my sisters, and between our parents. That's the role I've always fulfilled and that's what, to a degree, has subsequently formed a large part of my character.

Niamh, 40, youngest daughter

> I think being the youngest child has had a really important effect on my life. The good side was that being the youngest released me from the full weight of my parents' expectations, which weighed quite heavily on my sisters, particularly Siobhan. The bad side is that, instead of giving me a sense of independence and space to develop my character, I was always the baby of the family, looked after and fretted about. This was frustrating and constraining. It's hard to grow up when everyone treats you as a baby . . . It's hard to tell what nature is and what is nurture but I think I am less confident than my sisters, partly because I was always following them . . . Three siblings is a complicated number. It's quite likely that there's not going to be space for the last child to develop their own character independently of the others. I compare myself to my sisters frequently and probably in a way that's quite unfavourable to me, which doesn't do a lot for my self-esteem.

These three brief case studies (Hill, 2003) provide a very interesting perspective as to the effect the ordinal position has on children's behaviour and personality, contrary to what the majority of the parents think about it. What is perhaps more important is not what parents think about it, but how children perceive it and the effect that their (i.e. children's) perception has on their own personality and behaviour. We think, unwittingly, many parents confuse loving all their children the same with treating them the same.

For the reasons that have been outlined here, parents may think that they treat all their children alike. In reality they do not, and nor do their children think so.

EFFECT OF DIFFERENT SITUATIONS ON CHILDREN'S BEHAVIOUR

As stated previously, parents are often puzzled when they find that their child is a model pupil at school and very demanding at home, or vice versa. It is also not uncommon when a child is 'golden' when he is with his grandparents but awful when he is with his parents or in other situations. Fifteen-year-old Randy was completely out of control at home. He abused alcohol regularly and sometimes quite excessively, occasionally used drugs, and flew off the handle if he could not have his own way; he was completely a law unto himself. He was excluded from his school on a permanent basis, and on a few occasions had been involved with the police. The fact that he had to spend 4–5 hours in a dark police cell did not bother him. When asked by his mother how he felt being in the cell, his response to his mother was that he went off to sleep and it did not worry him at all. Because his own parents could not cope with him, he lived with his maternal grandparents. They were able to manage him and Randy had a close relationship with them. The way Randy behaved at his grandparents' home was very different to the way he behaved when he was with his parents. Equally, the way his grandparents treated him was considerably different to the way his own parents managed him.

Ten-year-old Danielle is another example. The school thought that she must have a 'split personality' because she denied having done something wrong in school even when a member of a staff had seen her doing it. Her head teacher firmly believed that she was not able to tell right from wrong. It was for these reasons that her school confidently believed that she must have schizophrenia. At home, parents found her a perfectly well behaved and sensible girl. These are just two examples of children behaving differently in different situations. It is not an uncommon occurrence.

When parents notice that their children behave differently in dissimilar situations, there is some variance in the way parents rationalise it. Some parents ascribe it to the fact that their child 'represses' his 'naughty' behaviour at school until he comes home. When he gets home he takes it out on his parents. Some parents think that it is further evidence that their child has a 'split personality'. Rarely would parents attribute it to the fact that the child is reacting to the way he is managed/treated in that situation.

When a child behaves differently in different situations, psychologists describe it as situation-specific behaviour:

> research on this question has produced evidence that both individual traits and situational variables influence behaviour. Some theorists emphasise consistency across situations; others stress situational influences. In line with their general emphasis on external influences, strong environmentalists stress situational determinants of behaviour. Therefore, they expect children to show little consistency across situations or stability over time unless the environment remains reasonably constant. People who stress biological bases for development and internal characteristics of the child tend to expect both consistency across situations and stability over time. (Mussen et al., 1990, p. 11)

We tend to favour that in many cases situations that people are in have a greater influence on the child's behaviour than biological factors and the internal characteristics of the child. Let us consider the case of Randy again. We have already mentioned that his behaviour at his maternal grandparents' house was much better compared to his own parents. Consider also the following situation, which shows how he is treated differently by different people in the same family and the effect it has on his feelings towards them. One evening Randy went to his parents' house and asked his mother if he could have a pound as he did not have any money. His mother said to him, in a somewhat aggressive way, 'no'; he could not have any because they were still paying a £150.00 fine to the court for what he had done. That money must come out of his pocket money. This is the only way he could learn, she said. Then Randy said if he could borrow a pound, he would try to pay her back. Again, the answer from her mother was an absolute 'no'. Randy obviously was not very pleased about this and he made a negative and somewhat derogatory remark about her and went away.

On the other hand, Randy's father one evening telephoned him and asked him if he would like to go for a drink at a pub and for a ride on his motorbike with him (it should be added that Mr S was advised that he should take his son out for a ride on his motorbike, given that Randy had been making exceptional efforts to change his behaviour and keep himself out of trouble). When Randy went with his father that evening, he bought him some cigarettes (Randy's parents knew that he was a habitual smoker and frequently drank alcohol whenever he had the opportunity to do so), a cigar and they had a drink together. Both Randy and his father enjoyed the evening together and it had a positive effect on their feelings towards each other, as reported by both of them when seen during subsequent sessions.

During the same week, when the above two incidents occurred, one with his mother and the other with his father, Randy's maternal grandmother won some money on the Pools. Without asking Randy, his Nan bought him a gold chain, topped up his mobile phone, bought him an expensive pair of jeans and some cigarettes.

The three brief interactions describe quite clearly how the same boy with the same awful history of deviant behaviour was treated differently by three different members of his family. Consequently, these different treatments elicited different responses from Randy towards these three different members of his family. As has already been mentioned above, Randy had extremely positive feelings for his maternal grandparents. He further added that he would do anything for them. His father accepted our advice and started to reward Randy more frequently, following serious efforts on Randy's part by not associating with the deviant peer group. This led Randy to have more affectionate feelings towards his father; about his mother, his passing comment was that she favoured his ten-year-old younger brother and had nothing positive to say about her. This is one of the many examples where we have noticed children responding differently to different situations by different members of the family. Hoffenaar and Hoeksma (2002), following their research, based on 1158 (560 boys and 598 girls) 8–12-year-old Dutch children came to the conclusion that a considerable part of children's oppositional behaviour was determined by the specific situation. They also found that the effect of situation is greater on girls than on boys; compared to boys, girls show less behaviour difficulties outside the family context.

To reiterate, in the light of what has been said above, parents need to be helped to fully appreciate that it is not unusual for children (or for that matter adults) to behave differently in different situations. If there is a variance in children's behaviours in different situations, it does not necessarily mean that they have either 'split personalities', or have inherited those traits. What it shows in the vast number of cases is that it is principally the effect of the situation that children are in, and the way people in those circumstances interact with them. Failure to address this, and the *other* issues that we have outlined in this chapter, can have a significant effect on the therapeutic outcome. It also, however, needs to be said, that some parents, despite clinicians' best efforts, are likely to remain wedded to their own belief system. Clinicians need to recognise and accept this reality when that happens.

Note

1. Professor Jay Belsky, Director of the Institute for the Study of Children, Families and Social Issues, Birkbeck College University of London

4

ESSENTIAL PRELIMINARIES AND SOME KEY POINTERS

INTRODUCTION

The preliminary considerations, and then the pointers that follow in this and the next chapter, are based on the experience of working with parents, and parents trying them out on their children (the first author trying some of them out as a parent). Further, they are grounded in well-researched psychological theory and empirical research. We consider them to be relevant and helpful to both clinicians and to parents as well (i.e. if the latter were reading the book). However, it needs to be noted that, except for a very small number of British Asian and British Black families, a vast majority of the families that we have seen were from disadvantaged backgrounds and were *white* indigenous families. We have intentionally highlighted the word 'white' to stress that we do not claim that our advice may be applicable to children and families across various cultures; we are saying this for the simple reason that they have not been tried on a large enough sample to make such a claim. What we can say is that they are likely to be and may require some modifications. However, were a clinician to try these ideas on families belonging to different cultural groups, should the ideas outlined here not work on them, it would be erroneous on the part of the clinician to blame the family and assume that they were not implementing the advice.

An alternative hypothesis should not be ruled out, i.e. that the advice given in this book is perhaps not applicable, or useful, to the member of that particular ethnic group. In this context, it is worth reminding ourselves of an often reported and interesting study by Deater-Deckard, Dodge, Bates & Pettit (1996). These researchers found that the use of physical punishment was associated with higher rates of antisocial behaviour among non-Hispanic white families, but not among African American families. A more recent study (Lansford, Deater-Deckard, Dodge, Bates & Pettit, 2004; see also studies cited therein) provides further support for these findings. The inference from this is that psychologists trained in psychology, which has a strong Western bias, should keep an open mind when applying its tenets to children raised in families who may have a different child-rearing perspective. This is chiefly because Eurocentric psychology may not provide the right interpretation of the situation and may not be generalisable across cultures (cf. d'Ardenne & Mahtani, 1999). In other words, clinicians giving advice on parenting need to take into account the cultural context of the families as well (Lansford et al., 2004).

ESSENTIAL PRELIMINARIES

1. These pointers, in most circumstances, expect parents to change their habitual approach of dealing with their children first, prior to asking children to make any changes in their behaviours (cf. Kazdin & Wassell, 2000b). Sometimes parents even wonder, how come all these demands are being made on them to change in their approach and not on their children first, who really are the problem – in so far as they are concerned, and what many parents often think and believe. Should not likewise some demands be made on children to demonstrate improved behaviour prior to asking parents to change the way they treat and manage their children? Common sense would dictate that should be the case. In reality, however, more often than not, it does not work that way, except in some circumstances. We are saying this because quite a few parents have raised this point with us.

   In a large majority of cases, the changes in parenting management style have to come from the parents first. The reason for this is that in line with other influential workers (e.g. Patterson, Reid & Dishion, 1992), our clinical experience shows that the majority of the behaviour problems of children in the home environment are often inadvertently developed, maintained and reinforced through maladaptive interactions between parents and children, though not often realised. With young children, parents are heavily involved; they are dispensers of positive and negative feedback to their children. This plays a critical role in shaping their behaviour. Consistent with this thinking, if the intervention is focused in reducing coercive or negative parenting interactions, not only will it improve the child's behaviour, but it will also reduce the stress on parents caused by their child's difficult behaviour, and improve the quality of their relationships.

   Mark's father, Robert, who used to be very aggressive towards his 15-year-old son, following our advice decided to change his interactional approach towards him. As a part of this change, Robert decided to be a little more laid-back, more accepting, more rewarding, and less punitive compared with what he used to be. He told us that as a result of bringing about this change in his own behaviour towards Mark, Robert had noticed a considerable change in Mark's attitude and behaviour towards his father. For instance, Mark had been very upset that a young girl, whom he fancied a lot, was not responding in the way he expected her to. Mark went to his father and asked if he could discuss a personal problem with him. Robert said that prior to changing his parenting style, Mark would never have discussed anything with him. Far from discussing anything with his father, Mark always made sure that he kept away from him and he gave him the feeling that he hated him. This brief vignette suggests that when parents are able to change their parenting style *first*, almost invariably, changes in children follow as well. We have witnessed this happening again and again.

2. It needs to be stated quite unequivocally that parents need to be willing, determined, motivated and consistent to implement these pointers to draw any real benefit from them. Trying them half-heartedly is not going to bring about any desirable results and often behaviour problems will actually worsen. Parents need to try these with an open mind. Perhaps we can say that this applies not only to our pointers but to any intervention strategy. Unless parents try it, they are unlikely to see any improvement in their child's behaviours.

   While these pointers are not claimed to be a panacea, having tried and tested them we can say with confidence that they are effective and they do help bring about changes in the child's behaviour and the family dynamics where parents have *implemented* them. The latter is a *sine qua non* for these to be of any help to parents (for other effective ways of helping parents see Scott, 2003; Hartman et al., 2003). Unlike some other studies which have looked into the benefits of their intervention beyond the referred child and the parents (e.g. Kazdin & Wassell, 2000b) we have not systematically questioned whether our intervention generalises to other members of the family, although many of them have reported significant improvements in the family dynamics.

3. It may be obvious to state, but it is very important that the parents fully understand the implications and ramifications of these pointers. Sometimes clinicians can erroneously think that parents have fully understood the advice given. But the reality is quite different. We can recall an interesting situation that illustrates this. It is related to advising parents to ignore trivial behaviours, which are not causing any damage to the property or hurting the child but are just annoying.

This advice was given during one of the sessions. When seen next time, the parents said that they were unable to implement it. The reason for not ignoring trivial behaviours was that they felt as if they were 'rejecting' their child. This was a complete misunderstanding of what was said in the session. Obviously, this was very instructive for us. It made us very aware of how certain pointers which may seem so obvious to a clinician can be quite difficult concepts for parents to grasp and therefore may require far more elucidation than a clinician might think.

4. It is acknowledged that some of these pointers may be perceived as not easy to put into action, and some may be seen as even more difficult than others to implement. It has already been observed above that these do make a considerable demand on the parents. One of the reasons for this is that successful implementation on the part of the parent requires a dual process: unlearning the old ways of dealing with the problem behaviour, and learning somewhat different and new approaches. For instance, a parent who, previously, had become annoyed each time their child misbehaved, may be asked to ignore trivial behaviours and not get worked up. Not only do they need to be familiar with the new approaches, they need to learn them again and again to ensure that they can use them with confidence, can generalise them across different situations and also that they do not regress to their old ways of behaving. Further, all this takes time and willingness to adopt and implement different strategies. What is true of adults having to unlearn and learn something new applies equally to children as well and this is taken up a little later.

It should also be noted that when parents do change and put into practice some of the pointers outlined here, they do witness significant improvement in their children's behaviour and interactions: children become relatively less confrontational and because of this improvement, the family dynamics become less stressful. Later on in the book, we will give a few examples of such changes that have taken place following implementation of some of these pointers. Thus these pointers may make demands on parents initially but when they (parents) do change in order to put into action some of these ideas, they undoubtedly notice that they experience significantly less 'grief' from their children. In other words, their initial efforts to change are amply rewarded.

5. It is important for parents to recognise that a lot of what they are doing is not helping the child to behave the way they want him to. If it did, they would not have needed to see the clinician. If they carry on using the strategies that have not worked, and are not working, they cannot expect any change in their child's behaviour. The situ-

ation can be compared with taking some medicine. If one knows that one has tried a particular medicine over a period and it has not worked, there is little point in carrying on with it. One would need to change the medicine to see if the new drug works. Likewise, if a parent has tried grounding for years or used shouting and knows it does not work, they need to look at alternatives that work.

6. Consistency and patience on the part of the parents are vitally important. It is no good implementing advice given one day and not the next day. It does not help the child to learn appropriate behaviour, if one day a child is punished or ignored for that behaviour, and the next day he is positively reinforced for the same behaviour either by giving in or by paying attention. This type of inconsistency makes it very difficult to develop a stable value system for guiding his behaviour. Both parents need to implement the advice as well.

7. Parents must realise that the behaviour is not going to change overnight. Equally, they must also appreciate that there is going to be some regression both on the part of the parents as well as on the part of the child. Sometimes, parents become complacent and go back to their old ways of interacting with the child. When that happens, the child too can return to his old ways of behaving, making the parent feel that what they are doing is just not working. They may start thinking that the advice given by the clinician was not working.

8. If by using some of the advice given here, parents have witnessed some improvement in their child's behaviour, it can be safely inferred that it is effective. The reason for the regression in the child's behaviour could lie elsewhere. It is feasible that the parents have unwittingly started paying attention to the undesirable patterns of behaviours and stopped ignoring them; or, they have started to reinforce the undesirable behaviours that did begin to show some improvement. Clinicians need to dissuade parents from forming a view that it is no good trying because their child's behaviour has gone back to square one again. What is needed here is that in conjunction with their clinician they need to examine and analyse the situation to see why the child has regressed despite showing some improvement at the beginning when they introduced these pointers. This process of improvement and regression in behaviour is somewhat analogous to dieting, or anything where one has to try to unlearn an old behaviour and learn something new. For successful dieting, people have to change their old and established eating pattern. They have to either stop or modify eating what they were used to previously, and learn to *stick* to eating different types of food. Many of us who have tried to diet must have experienced that we often relapse back into the old ways of eating. During this process, many of us get fed up, as we do

not seem to be getting anywhere and give up altogether. A process similar to dieting can happen in efforts to implement these pointers. Parents need to be made aware of that.

9. It is not expected that you will agree with all the pointers outlined here. It is up to the individual reader which ones they pick and choose and advise parents to implement. It is not suggested that parents should implement all of them. Clinicians, in consultation with the parents, should help them in deciding which ideas are likely to be helpful in their situation. It is recommended that one or two ideas at a time are introduced and that the clinician is then guided by the feedback that they get as a result of introducing them. Surprisingly, sometimes the implementation of one or a few of the pointers can help alleviate the problem. In the case of eight-year-old Connor, his mother was extremely stressed by his behaviour and following our advice she introduced one of the pointers. The pointer was that if she was going to say 'yes' to her child's demand eventually, why not say it in the first place? Following this advice, when she was seen again, she reported considerable improvement in his behaviour. Additionally, it had a positive effect on her own mental well-being and she felt more positively about Connor as well (see the section 'Reduce avoidable confrontations' on p. 57, where the details of this pointer are discussed further).

10. Parents' feeling guilty that they have failed does not help; or, that they are instrumental for their child's bad behaviour does not help either, although there may be some truth in the latter (see e.g. bidirectionality about parental contribution to the interactional difficulties that they have with their children). Additionally, it is also worth bearing in mind the problems that are generated for these families by the complex circumstances that they are in. This may include broken marriages and problems following from that even years after splitting up or divorce; problems which stem from their new relationships; financial difficulties; and the difficulties of the neighbourhood where some of the referred families live. Further, circumstances such as these and the oppositional, aggressive and deviant behaviours that the referred child presents may result in his having to leave his home and start living with his grandparents. This often makes the mother guilty and the child resentful towards his mother. All these difficulties that we have alluded to here were seen in the case of 16-year-old Christopher whom we briefly mentioned in an earlier chapter.

The pointers that follow are intended to be practical and accessible to the clinician and to the parents. Where it is felt that reference to a case would help to illustrate a point, necessary and relevant details of a case have been provided. In writing these pointers, the guiding principal for us has been, would it help the parent if they were reading them? For a clinician, reference to such vignettes may or may not be necessary. With some pointers where we felt it was not necessary to elucidate by referring to a case study, no reference to any vignettes has been made. There are a number of pointers which have required considerably longer treatment, for example: parents should look after themselves; they need to set a good example; the role of self-concept and so on. They have not been numbered with the rest but have been described under appropriate subheadings, e.g. 'Importance of Parents' Own Emotional Well-Being' and so on.

POINTERS

Importance of Parents' Own Emotional Well-Being

Most parents would know that children's temper tantrums, aggressive and non-compliant behaviours, moodiness, sulkiness, bad attitude, violent outbursts and so on can be emotionally and physically draining. When they have to deal with such behaviours day in and day out, parents understandably feel psychologically and physically shattered, drained, and stressed. During clinical sessions a very high percentage of parents report that. As an example, a 43-year-old mother of two children with behaviour problems, aged five and three, said to us that when she feels totally weary and emotionally and physically worn out because of her children's behaviour problems, her way of coping with her emotional state is to leave her children downstairs and go and hide herself in her en suite bathroom.

The wear and tear, as a result of the conflicts that parents have with their children, and the manner in which they deal with them, are greater on them than on children. Some parents experience more stress following their children's oppositional behaviours than others. Based on our observations as to why some parents suffer more stress than others, some of the reasons which appear to be common to many parents are:

1. These parents tend to be very short tempered and become very easily annoyed if their children do not do as they are told.
2. These parents take much longer to recover from the state of emotional arousal than children.
3. These parents continue to harbour feelings of irritation and annoyance against the child for a much longer period than children.
4. Often these parents have unrealistic expectations of their children in terms of their behaviours which are not commensurate with their age,

ability and aptitude (cf. Chess & Thomas, 1999). We return to this topic again later in this book, as we have found that many parents repeatedly make this mistake and consequently it leads to so many problems with their children.

5. Often these parents tend to lay all the blame on to their children and refuse to see how they could be contributing to the problems that they are having with their children (for more details see 'Attribution errors' (p. 9) and 'Bi-directionality' (p. 30).

6. Often these parents are quite authoritarian in their approach and resent having to do things for their children.

Come the end of the day, the cumulative effect on parents of antagonistic situations between them and children, which may arise several times during the day, is very tiring and exasperating. This is true of a very high percentage of the families that we see. However, in focusing our discussion concerning the stress which many parents experience following their interactions with their children, we are not suggesting that this invariably is the only source of stress for them (for other sources of stress on parents, see also Sidebotham, 2001).

The extent to which the stress can have an effect on the way the parents interact with their children is not fully appreciated and recognised by many parents and some clinicians as well. Recognising and emphasising its importance, Rhodes (2003) says 'that behavioural intervention for severe problem behaviour in children with intellectual disabilities [in our experience that this applies irrespective of any particular kind of disability] is most successful when family issues including stress have been addressed *preintervention*' (emphasis added; cited in Hastings & Beck, 2004, p. 1339). This view echoes our clinical practice fully where we routinely address issues which concern parents as well. Thus, if clinicians were to incorporate parent issues in their treatment plan, not only does it improve the outcome, but according to Kazdin, Holland & Crowley (1997) it also reduces the chances of parents dropping out of the treatment as well.

When parents are feeling stressed, they easily become annoyed, fed up and irritated with their children. In that frame of mind, even children's minor departures from acceptable behaviours can appear magnified to them. These feelings of negativity make parents feel even more *stressed*. Invariably, when parents feel harassed, they deal with their children in a way that only exacerbates the situation. This can be presented schematically as shown in Figure 4.1.

As this figure shows, this sets up a vicious cycle between children and parents that needs to be broken. If it is not broken, both parents and children will go round and round, making things worse for each other. On

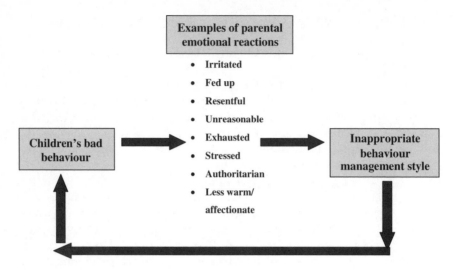

Figure 4.1 Schematic representation of interaction between children's behaviour and its adverse effect on parenting style

the other hand, when parents are quite relaxed in their approach, they are able to deal with their children in such a way that it often does not escalate the situation (or get out of control), thereby making it worse for the children and parents: in fact, almost all the parents when asked invariably confirm this. A mother of six-year-old Jelani said that when she was angry and frazzled, she did not deal with his annoying behaviour at that time. This was because she had realised that under those circumstances she would be unduly aggressive and unreasonable with him. When she reacted that way towards Jelani, his behaviour got worse and that caused his mother a lot of stress. In view of this, the approach that she adopted was that she would allow herself to calm down *first* and then she would deal with him. She found this way of dealing with him much better for him and for her as well.

It is therefore crucially important that parents adopt strategies conducive to reducing their stress when they normally interact with their children's various demands, and also try to cope with their non-compliant and difficult behaviours. If they are able to achieve that, it would be in the best interests of the child and parents. This also means that parents would need to tackle children's behaviours differently compared to the way they had been habitually dealing with them previously, which has been one of the causes of their difficult behaviour and which has caused parents a lot of stress as well. Clinicians, however, need to bear in mind that for parents to change their habitual ways of reacting is not that simple and does not happen overnight. As well as the need to be convinced that they should change their customary parenting style, parents also need to learn the new approach.

It is as a result of our becoming acutely aware of the importance of parental stress and its adverse effect on their interactions with their children that we have used the following ideas which we have found helpful in reducing their stress levels and, in turn, improving their parenting style and their relationship with their children.

Reduce avoidable confrontations

Some confrontations with children are unnecessary and, with a little tact on the part of parents, can be avoided; and this should, as well as enhancing the quality of relationship between children and parents, also reduce the stress on them which these situations often generate. In this section, therefore, we look at some of the strategies that parents can employ when they are dealing with provocative situations with their children and which, with some parents, can frequently arise.

If parents observe their own behaviours they would notice that there are times when their child has made a demand, or asked them to do something, and they have said 'no' without really thinking about it. This response is often a force of habit; they could easily have said 'yes', instead of 'no'. If they had done that, that would have avoided quite a few unnecessary confrontations during the day. Thus our first pointer is that when children make various demands on parents, they should try to say 'yes', if they can. Not only should they say 'yes' but this should be done with good grace and not grudgingly. This point gets further elaborated, and hopefully clarified, as we go along in this section.

While we were explaining this point (saying 'yes' when parents *can* instead of saying 'no') to a 28-year-old single mother (Tracey) of a seven-year-old daughter who used to show a lot of anger towards her mother, Tracey herself gave us an example of such a situation. Tracey was doing her hair and Sam, her daughter, asked her mother if she could get a toy down which was too high for her to reach. Her mother said to Sam that she should wait, until she had finished doing her hair. Sam started kicking a fuss and this small incident led to a big battle between Mum and Sam. Mum had to stop doing her hair and she ended up getting Sam the toy down. During the session, Tracey reflected and said that had she got Sam her toy down in the *first place*, she would have avoided an unnecessary conflict. She further added that she said 'no' without really thinking about it. As we consider this point to be very important in helping parents to reduce their stress, we provide below a few more examples.

It is breakfast time. When asked, the child does not want to eat anything that is normally eaten at breakfast time, e.g. toast, some cereal or eggs. He says that he wants some soup. Should a parent have a confrontation and say 'no', that he could not have it because it was silly and people normally do not eat soup at breakfast time? Before we offer our views, let us take two more examples and then we will return to each one by one. The child needs a bath or a shower today. The parent thinks that he must have it tonight. The child says 'no' and says that he did not want it tonight but would have it the next day without any fuss. Should a parent insist that the child must have it tonight because she has said so? Yet another illustration of such a situation, which can give rise to a conflict, is that a parent has asked a six-year-old child to go and get dressed. The child gets dressed but chooses clothes which do not match, or of which the parent does not approve. When a parent points this out to the child, she insists that she likes those clothes and would like to keep them on. Should you make the child change her clothes even when the parent knows that they have no plans to go out, nor are they expecting anybody to come?

Let us now take each of the above examples in turn. Does it matter if the child has soup in the morning, although conventionally people do not eat it? Soup has some food value, it does not take any longer to cook or eat (we are assuming that one has some soup in the house) than a piece of toast or some cereal. Is there any point in saying 'no' to the child that he could not have soup because traditionally people do not have soup in the morning? Likewise, does it matter if the child has a shower in the morning instead of tonight, if he is going to have it in the morning without any fuss? Are parents insisting that he must have a shower tonight because it is a matter of routine and often he has it at night time? With the third example too, our reaction is that it hardly matters if a child is allowed to wear clothes of his choice, as he is not going out nor any guests expected. Our view is that in each of the three cases it is best to go along with the child's wishes rather than create a conflicting situation with the child, bearing in mind that each conflict a parent has with the child generates its own stress, more for the parent than for the child.

Thus our advice in each case that we gave to parents was that they should say 'yes' – and gracefully – and not make the child feel that he was being silly for making unconventional demands. We must add that a very high percentage of the parents begin to see our logic and thinking behind this when we have explained this point to them. They begin to see that they had been inflexible in their approach, had unrealistic expectations, and made an issue of trivial things, as the following case study illustrates.

Brady, a nine-year-old boy, was referred to us by his family doctor. His family doctor wrote that Brady's parents were becoming anxious about his behaviour at home and school. He had outbursts of bad behaviour and tantrums and refused to accept disciplining measures. He had been getting into trouble at school as well. He lived with his parents and two older sisters. There had been no domestic upheavals. He had also been getting migraine headaches.

During the first consultation, some of the things that his parents said about his behaviour were: that he lost his temper quickly; he had no consideration towards people, although he was described as kind to animals; if parents said 'no' to anything, he reacted aggressively and violently. If he got what he wanted, he was all right. Often, he behaved well, when he went and saw his grandparents. He had two older brothers, aged 14 and 15, whose behaviour on the whole was satisfactory.

Both parents worked and came home tired. They had little time for him and it appeared to us that they had somewhat unrealistic expectations of him, which were not commensurate with his age and ability. Mum described herself as stricter than his father and 'nagged' over trivial things. From this and the other information given, the advice given was that they should try to say 'yes' when they could, instead of saying 'no'. It was better to say 'yes' in the first place rather than saying 'yes' after he had been pestering them, so that they got some peace and quiet. The advantages and why this approach was useful and helpful in reducing their stress level and improving the quality of their relationship were carefully explained to them.

Mr and Mrs S, out of politeness, did not say to us what they really felt about this advice. When they came for the second session, they told us that when they went home after the first session, they had mocked the advice given to them. Despite their initial, somewhat light-hearted view about this advice, they still implemented it. When they returned for their second appointment, some of their comments about the effectiveness of this pointer included: 'very pleased with the progress'. The way he had behaved during the last two weeks or so, it seemed that they did not have any problem with him any more. More importantly, Mr and Mrs S also made the following observations:

1. They saw the benefits of saying 'yes' when they could, instead of saying 'no', and then saying 'yes' if he continued to persevere in his demands. They said that as a result of following this technique, they had far fewer confrontations with him compared with what they normally used to have. A positive consequence of this was that it reduced their stress levels and improved their quality of interactions with him.

2. They recognised that they used to be impatient with him and had unrealistic expectations of him in terms of his behaviour, i.e. they expected him to behave in a more mature and grown-up manner compared with his actual age and ability.
3. It helped the parents to recognise that it was they who needed to modify their own behaviour towards their son and it also made them realise that they needed to bring about some changes in their previous habitual parenting style.

Confusing saying 'yes' with giving in

However, a small percentage of the parents do confuse this type of approach with giving in. This approach does not mean that the parents have given in to the whims of the child and have given him the upper hand, as some of them tend to believe. Giving in is different from saying 'yes' in the first place, if a parent is going to say 'yes' eventually following their child's perseverance with their demands. With giving in, what happens is that a child asks for something; the parent says 'no'; then the child starts going on and on; a parent gets fed up and cannot 'take any more', and then gives in to his demands and ends up saying 'yes' and also in a most ungracious manner. Saying 'yes' under those circumstances does not have the same effect on the child as saying 'yes' in the first place. We reiterate that we are not advancing the view that parents should say 'yes' to the child's each and every reasonable or unreasonable demand; the emphasis here is that they should say 'yes' when it is feasible for them to do so. When the child ends up having his own way as a result of his being adamant and parents giving in, each is left nursing unpleasant and often strong negative feelings for each other. It does not make the child appreciate that, after all, his parents have let him have what he wanted and therefore he should show some appreciation to his parents. Frequent occurrence of such negative feelings towards each other results in a hostile relationship between parents and children in the long run. It needs to be emphasised to parents that the development and maintenance of such a situation needs to be avoided at all costs. Our pointer that if parents can say 'yes' in the first place rather than saying 'no' and then 'yes', positively helps in reducing negative feelings and promotes positive feelings for each other. In addition to this, there are several other benefits which are outlined in the section below.

In one case, where we felt that a parent did not understand, or chose not to understand, this strategy she went and consulted one of her friends about this advice. Our client's friend agreed with her and when she came back and saw us the next time, she gave us the impression that we had gone mad and did not know what we were talking about! Fortunately, such a response is an infrequent occurrence. Interestingly, when one does come across such parents, they often come over as very authoritarian and inflexible in their parenting style – a not very helpful approach in dealing with children.

Benefits of this approach

There are a number of benefits when parents implement what we are advocating here, i.e. saying 'yes' in the first place when they possibly can, instead of no; this applies not only to the case studies that we have described, but to the others that follow as well.

1. Returning to our soup scenario again, as well as saying 'yes', a parent can also explain that he could have it but normally it is not eaten at breakfast time. However, if the child were in a situation where it was unacceptable to let him have it for whatever reason, he would not be allowed to do so. It is highly probable that the child would accept and conform when it is necessary to do so, hopefully without being oppositional. By adopting this stance, a parent is somewhat indirectly helping the child to appreciate how certain behaviours are acceptable in certain situations and during certain times; on the other hand, there are also situations when they are unacceptable. It is an important thing to learn; however, parents should be assisted in realising that children do not learn this concept overnight, or with one example only. This is because, as we all know, we learn through the course of our lives that we do have to behave differently in different situations. For instance, as adults we know that the type of diction we use in informal situations is different from the language we would use during an interview, or if we were meeting somebody formally. Similarly, it is acceptable to wear pyjamas in the house when you are on your own and not when you have visitors around.

2. By going along with the child's reasonable demands when it is possible for parents to do so, they are giving children the feeling that they do not always say 'no' for the sake of it. Many young adults that we interview often say to us how unreasonable their parents are as they never say 'yes', particularly when they think that they could have, and to what appears to them to be a reasonable request. While it is not the only reason, children start developing resentment towards parents if they believe that they say 'no' all the time to them. We feel that it is quite serious when children develop feelings of bitterness towards their parents. We have seen on several occasions disdainful

expressions on the faces of the children when they either look at their parents or talk to them. We could almost see intense hatred in the eyes of the child towards his parents. To shift from such an extreme position to a point where the child has feelings of love and respect is quite a hard task for the child, the parents and the clinician. It is therefore better that the relationship does not reach that level in the first place. Surely, parents do not say 'no' all the time, but a child can develop this type of impression, perhaps sometimes somewhat erroneously. It is therefore very important that parents do not unwittingly end up giving the impression to their children that they are always saying 'no' to them and have a relationship which is less than warm and affectionate. However, more often than not, we have found that where parents have implemented this approach, it has helped to improve children's perception of them as being unjust and difficult to deal with, as it has also helped to improve their relationship with them.

3. Parents who say 'no' excessively give the feeling to the child that they are very inflexible and also perhaps authoritarian. By behaving that way, parents are setting a bad example for their children (we discuss this point at a greater length again under the headings 'Imitation in childhood/observational learning' (p. 85) and 'Modelling' (p. 86). In other words, children also learn from parents to say 'no' when they are asked to do anything. When children say 'no' to parents, the parents do not like it and feel annoyed with them, which leads to a conflict situation between them. The more conflicts parents have with their children, the more damage occurs in their relationship.

Now we turn to some other ways of reducing hostile encounters between children and parents and thus reducing the stress that such conflicts produce on parents and that impair the quality of their relationship.

- Yet another way of reducing confrontations with children is to learn to ignore some of their minor aggravating behaviours. Sometimes parents react to even small irrational behaviours and allow themselves to get all worked up. Such insignificant behaviours, no matter how annoying (so long as the child is not hurting himself or anybody else, or causing any damage) are best ignored. Ignoring bad behaviour is not the same as parents ignoring their child, although sometimes some parents do tend to think that way.
- Avoid triggers which often lead to flare-ups. Fourteen-year-old Esther had moderate learning difficulties and was overall functioning at around the-six-year old level. She was often asked numerous questions about her school day as she walked into the house by her well-meaning single mother who had been sitting in the house all day by herself. These questions (which Esther was unable to answer because of

her limited linguistic ability and which her mother failed to appreciate) acted as a trigger which often resulted in such behaviours as going to her bedroom in a sulky mood, and banging doors while going upstairs. For the rest of the evening, she shut herself in her bedroom and it spoiled the rest of the evening both for her and her mother who in a way had been looking forward to Esther coming home. The way Mrs B, Esther's mother, dealt with her behaviour on return from school was to stop using the trigger (i.e. asking questions) which was instrumental in causing the rift between mother and daughter. Instead, we advised her that as soon as Esther was dropped by her taxi and she came into the house, rather than asking her any questions, there should be a drink and something to eat (which she enjoyed eating) for her on the table. We also encouraged Mrs B to leave it to Esther to tell her about her school day when she was ready to do so.

- When parents have to be confrontational, they should try to remain as calm as possible. They should also learn to recognise the first signs of anger which can lead to explosion. When they feel that happening, they should give themselves a signal, such as: 'here we go again'. It is time for them to stop and not make the situation worse. The spin off of this would be less emotional wear and tear on the parents and they would be able to deal with annoying behaviours much more effectively. Sometimes this is recognised by parents themselves and they do not need telling. A 54-year-old father, who himself admitted (and his wife confirmed) that he was quick to react, added that whenever he managed to ignore his 13-year-old son's extremely rude and hurtful behaviour, not only did his son not react, but also came to him afterwards and apologised. A very similar observation was made by the father of a 14-year-old daughter.

- Parents should not miss any opportunity when they can sit and relax and recharge their batteries. This could be when a toddler is asleep or the school-aged child has gone to school or to play outside. Parents should not feel guilty in doing this, or that they ought to be occupied in doing some jobs in the house and not just sitting doing nothing and relaxing. Parents need to be helped to recognise that no one can be on the go and doing things all the time. More importantly, if they are less worn out, they would be in a much better position to cope with any confrontational situations which may arise from time to time. Time and again parents confirm how they react differently when they still have a reasonable amount of energy and patience left in them.

- Although by no means easy to implement when tempers are high, humour can diffuse the situation and can almost stop it from escalating when a parent is feeling angry with the child. However, it should not be either belittling or at the expense of the child.

- Parents need to be flexible in dealing with their children. Inflexible rules in the house do not help and they simply lead to arguments between children and parents. For instance, as soon as the child walks into the house from school, some parents insist that they must take their school uniform off before they are allowed to do anything else. Rules need to be interpreted somewhat liberally and not literally. The aim behind these rules is not to catch the child breaking them but to give him the impression that he follows them. If, with the assistance of his parents, a child develops a self-concept that he is good at following rules, it is better than if he starts believing that he is not good at following rules (please see the section under the heading 'Role and development of self-concept' (p. 82) for a discussion on how our perception of ourselves can influence behaviour). There is then a greater probability that he would try and follow rules than break them. It is equally better to err on the side of having a few essential or important rules, rather than numerous minor rules.

- Taking issue over trivial things should be avoided at all costs. The problem arises when what is perceived to be trivial by the child is important for the parent. When something is considered to be unimportant, it invariably does not stay in our memory, irrespective of how often we are reminded. An example of such a situation that frequently arises between children and parents is when the former do not put their school bags and shoes away on return from school, despite the fact that parents have asked and reminded their children on countless occasions. If parents learn not to ignore it, or continue to make it into a big issue when the child returns from school, this can turn into an unpleasant encounter between the child and the parents almost every evening. The bad feelings for each other arising from such a daily occurrence can have repercussions for the rest of the evening. Because of this unpleasant incident, both parents and children can continue to harbour negative feelings for each other for a considerable period of time. Should another disagreement occur later on in the evening, tempers may flare up more easily because both children and parents may still be nursing their earlier grievance and annoyance with each other. Such repeated unpleasant and disagreeable incidents are not a good recipe for harmonious and desirable relationships between parents and children, and they stress parents out.

In situations like this, some of the options that parents have can be summarised as follows:

1. Perhaps the most difficult to implement is: *without getting worked up*, to continue to ask their children to put their school items away when they have not done so.
2. Parents would feel less irritated if they were able to accept and recognise that the task they are asking their children to do is inconsequential, possibly, as perceived by them. In view of this, they are likely to keep forgetting it. If parents do want those things to be put away they can keep reminding them and asking them nicely about it, as has also been noted in (1). We accept that it is not a strategy that many parents would conventionally use.
3. To go out of the way to ensure that they reward children when they do put things away. Equally, they need to accept that because they have put their stuff away once, they might not put it away the next day. Unless the new behaviour is fully mastered, it is unlikely that they would consistently do it.
4. To continue as they have been doing and facing the consequences; i.e. having an unpleasant encounter over this or similar issues each time they occur and suffering the stress arising from this.

Obviously, our recommendation to parents is that they should try and deal with it in such a way that it causes them a minimum amount of stress and is not detrimental to their relationship with their children. We consider that it is of paramount importance that parents continue to maintain a good relationship despite the fact that they have difficulties with their children. Clearly, parents should not try to create an impression on their children that they just nag as soon as they walk into the house.

• Parents should try and anticipate 'disasters', if they can, and plan ahead to tackle them. As well as this being common sense, there is some research evidence which has shown some relationship between parents taking proactive steps and reduction in behaviour problems (Denham, Workman, Cole, Weissbrod, Kensziora & Zahan-Waxler, 2000; Gardner, Sonuga-Barke & Syal, 1999). Take, for instance, when parents have to go and see their doctor or have to be in a situation where they have to wait. In circumstances like these, more often than not, the child is going to get bored. It would be totally unrealistic on the part of the parents if they expect that their child should not get bored and ought to behave. A bored child is likely to be demanding, difficult and possibly would behave in a way likely to cause embarrassment to the parents. This could be avoided if the parent went prepared with an interesting book or with a few toys which are likely to occupy them while they are waiting to be seen. However, parents ought to recognise that under these circumstances, they should not expect that the child is going to be an angel!

Perhaps another scenario about nine-year-old Bradley would further help elucidate this point regarding planning ahead. His case has been mentioned elsewhere in the book as well. Just to briefly remind you, the reason for his referral was that he presented behaviour problems at home. During one of the sessions when his mother came to see us, she said that apart from this morning, on the whole his behaviour had been good. When asked what happened that morning, Mrs H said that he was abusive towards her. The reason for this was that he did not want to wear his T-shirt which had a tight-fit style. He had six of those and he had previously told his mother that he did not like them; they were out of fashion and he would rather be seen dead than alive in those T-shirts. He had four T-shirts which were loose fitting, the type he liked, the type most boys he thought wore. His mother knew about his preferred T-shirts, but the morning of the incident, all his loose T-shirts were dirty; only the tight-fitting T-shirts were clean. This had happened several times before, i.e. when his mother did not have the T-shirt he liked ready for him to wear. In addition to that, his mother had an appointment to come and see us. The implication of the latter was that she did not have much time in the morning to deal with him compared to when she was not going out anywhere in the morning.

Ideally, it would be highly desirable if Bradley had understood his mother's position and for that morning wore the T-shirt that was available and not kicked up a fuss. Perhaps many parents would share that view. However, this was unlikely to happen because, in the past too, when his preferred T-shirt had not been ready, he had gone off the rails. We tend to favour the view that, if Mum had already experienced the consequences of not having the T-shirt ready, we would say that she should have gone out of her way to ensure that it was ready for the following morning, especially since his recent behaviour had been generally good. Some parents may interpret our standpoint that it is like giving in to the child's whims. We do not think so. Our reasoning of why Mum should have taken the trouble to have the T-shirt ready is as follows.

1. First, the relationship between Bradley and his mother was already fraught. It is an important consideration that because of this, he would be unlikely to go along to please his mother by agreeing to wear whichever T-shirt was ready.
2. It may be unrealistic (please see our views on 'Realistic expectations' (p. 79) to expect Bradley to be able to see from his mother's perspective.
3. His mother is not seeing from his point of view how for him it is important to wear clothes which are currently fashionable and what impact it was likely to have on his self-esteem.

4. It would have avoided the unpleasant episode which had a stressful effect on his mother.
5. Bradley might infer that his mother does not care what he likes and does not like.

We hope this example of Bradley further illustrates our point that we should try to plan ahead and try to avoid disasters which have a stressful effect on the parents and are bad for the relationships between the child and the parents.

- Another situation that is often frustrating and annoying for parents and which is a great source of stress for them is when they have to go shopping with their children. On the one hand, parents have to do the shopping. On the other hand, the experience of shopping with parents is deadly boring for most children, particularly when it becomes a long expedition – at least that is how the child might see it! Parents who think that children ought to be able to cope with this, or ought to understand that shopping has to be done, are likely to be disappointed. It is highly unlikely that many children, unless they happen to be extremely compliant, will be able to cope; few would be able to demonstrate the type of awareness that parents may expect their child to show, e.g. if Mum did not buy food, there won't be food in the house to eat. Instead of showing this type of understanding, chances are that their thinking is likely to be determined by their self-centred feelings that it is boring for them. Under the circumstance, what can parents do so that they do not experience too much stress? We outline below some of the options that we have suggested to parents.

1. Perhaps the first option is that parents try to make the shopping session as brief as possible.
2. They should also be acutely aware that it is likely to be boring for the child and think about what they can do beforehand to make it less tedious for the child. We think the child's perspective is best understood if parents were able to put themselves into the child's shoes and see how he perceives and interprets the shopping experience (do not expect that the child will be able to see from your perspective – for details see the section 'Realistic expectations' (p. 79). Putting it in a different way, imagine if the parents were dragged along by the child from one shop to another which had no interest whatsoever for them and they had nobody to talk to.
3. They need to be mentally prepared that their child may present some problems and they should try not to get worked up.
4. Where it is possible, perhaps the easiest strategy is that the child is left with the other partner and only one parent goes shopping. We

appreciate that there can be circumstances where a parent may not have a partner. Perhaps under those circumstances, one of the other options suggested could be tried.

Parents need to recognise that time pressures cause considerable stress on them (Sidebotham, 2001). They cannot be on top of everything every day and complete what they had planned to do. What is planned for the day needs to be comfortably achievable. In that plan, they must include the time required for meeting their children's demands, as well as time for playing and doing things for them. If this means postponing less important things to another day, so be it. Little purpose would be served if they felt guilty because they had not achieved what they had set out to accomplish for that day.

- It is also well to recognise that parents will not be able to achieve as much as when they did not have the children. This includes housework; they may not be able to keep their house as immaculate as they were able to maintain or would like it to be. It does not mean that one has to live in squalor.
- Parents may wish it, they may desire it, but the children are not easily going to fit in with their lifestyle. The more they expect it, the more it is likely to lead to conflicts between parents and children. Remember, each time they have a conflict with the child, each time it can and often does drain parents' energy and leaves them feeling awful and angry with the child. They will have to make adjustments to accommodate their difficult and demanding children in line with their age, ability and emotional development. It does not mean pandering to the wishes of the child. Such an approach will reduce confrontations with the child.
- Parents will be disappointed if they expect unquestioning and immediate obedience from their children when they give them any commands, e.g. 'I am asking you to put it away *now*' or, 'Stop *straight away* what you are doing and get ready.' Such commands are better phrased as: 'Would you like to put your things away for me when you have finished with what you are doing?' In taking this approach, parents are conveying to the child that they value and appreciate what the child is doing. If the child procrastinates, parents should be prepared to accept it rather than feel 'How dare he not do it straight away?' Equally, if the child forgets to do what he had been asked to do, it is better not to get worked up about it. Remember, what is important to parents may not be important to the child. For instance, it may be important for the parent that the room looks tidy but may not be important to the child. As emphasised previously, what is not important is often forgotten; this applies to the child as well as to the adult.

- During the day, parents have to attend to a number of jobs. They are often pushed for time. In planning, or wanting, to do all the jobs in a day, they often do not make allowances for things not going as intended (e.g. a child may have a temper tantrum for some reason or other, and may require some time to be dealt with; a child may not get ready as quickly in the morning as they would like him to). This may upset their plans; they are late for school or for an appointment, or for work. All this can cause a lot of stress. There are three possible options to deal with such unforeseen eventualities.

1. Mental preparedness that everything may not go as planned. Such a mental attitude is less likely to cause as much stress as when one is caught unprepared.
2. Allow a little more time for each job; this is especially important in the mornings when so many things need to be juggled around by the parents, particularly working mothers who are trying to combine several roles. Such a suggestion may not be acceptable to some parents. They may argue about why they should get up earlier than they have to, just because the child does not do things as he ought to. If parents adhere to that line of reasoning (and unfortunately many parents do), they are going to be disappointed. This is because many children are not going to do what parents expect them to do, if the expectations are not commensurate with their age, emotional and cognitive development (please also refer to the section on 'Realistic expectations', p. 79). A six-year-old child is not going to appreciate that he should get ready himself and show an understanding that if he did not, his mother would be late for work; if she is late for work, her boss is not going to be very happy with her. If this continues to happen repeatedly, she might lose her job, or be in trouble. If she lost her job, the family won't have as much money as they have now, and so on. The consequence of such a choice of an unrealistic expectation on the part of the parent would be that they get irritated with their children and stressed. This makes the situation worse for all concerned. We were discussing this point with a colleague who expected her pre-school child to get ready by herself in the mornings. This colleague's belief was that her child was old enough to get ready independently without requiring much assistance from her. Every morning she had a 'battle' with her in that she expected her child to get ready with little assistance from her mother, and she would not. That resulted in the child feeling unhappy and the mother feeling highly stressed and annoyed with her. Following this colleague's discussion with us, she started allowing a little more time and revised her expectations. The result of this change was

that she had far fewer problems in the morning and far less stress compared with what she used to experience before.

3. Sometimes a child would do something with less resistance, or comply more easily, if the parent offered something without having been asked by the child. Obviously, what is given, the child must *like* it (see 'Use of rewards/reinforcement' (p. 118) for details). For instance, before waking up the child in the morning, the parent could take a small drink for him. Thus, when the parent says to the child, it is time to get up, the parent could say: 'Come on, here is a drink for you and when you have had the drink, then get up.' (In a similar situation, some parents have used a few sweets instead of a drink.) It is highly probable that with this approach, the child is likely to present less resistance in getting up. If the child presents less struggle, this means it is less taxing for the parent. Obviously, both the parents and the child would need a little more time than usual. This is because the parent would need time to make the drink, take it to the child and the child would need time to finish it. While we claim that it is a helpful approach, it is equally important that parents should not expect it to be a miracle and because the child has been given a drink, they could expect perfect compliance for the rest of the morning, or the rest of the day. The target of this approach/treat is that the child, hopefully, gets up with relatively less resistance – and hence less stress for the parent than usual.

The approach described above can be used with children where parents often express annoyance that their child is in an awful mood when he comes back from school. It is not always easy to determine as to why the child arrives home in a fractious mood. This could be due to a number of reasons and possibly interactions among them as well. Nor is it worthwhile asking the child why he is in such a mood, for the simple reason that it is not likely that the parent would get any sensible response from the child. Not getting any answer from the child is only likely to annoy the parents.

When the child is in such a frame of mind, the situation is likely to become even worse when, as soon as the child walks into the house, he meets a command from his parents such as: 'Hang your coat up' or 'Put your bags and shoes away' or 'Change your school uniform' – a situation we have alluded to above as well, which is a frequent cause of aggravation between the parents and children.

We feel that it can be tackled in such a way that every day it does not become a time of conflict or battle for the parents and hence a stressful time. Before the child arrives, there could be a drink and/or something to eat ready for the child. When the child has had a drink and something to eat, perhaps a parent could *ask* then, if the child would help putting their things away or change their school uniform. Parents should remember that they are only *asking* and not *telling* the child to do something. This means they should be prepared to accept delay or refusal to do what he has been asked. Parents should also remember that hanging the child's coat up is less stressful than having a battle every evening when the child returns from school. The choice lies with the parent as to the option they decide to go for!

A few parents, and a colleague who read this chapter, have raised the question with regard to the strategy that we have described above: what about even if the parent has given a drink, or a sweet, or a small treat, and the child still does not get up or show less resistance? While it is undoubtedly possible that the child may not do what the parent has expected him to do, the majority of the parents, including the first author, who have tried this idea with his own children have found that it does help. With this approach, what one is doing is pairing concurrently something pleasant (say sweet) with something which is perceived as disagreeable (getting up) by the child (cf. the notion of reciprocal inhibition, Wolpe, 1958). By so doing, what seems to happen is that the child's extreme response either becomes diffused or weak. In other words, the child does not protest or present difficult behaviour to the same extent. And it is of considerable help to a harassed parent.

We acknowledge that this suggestion is against one of the key principles of psychology: that is, rewards should follow after the desired event and not before it. However, our approach does seem to have some similarities with the notion of non-contingent reinforcement which recent research has shown is an effective form of reinforcement in treating behaviour problems (Lalli, Casey & Kates, 1997). What seems to happen with non-contingent reinforcement is that it 'weakens the response-reinforcer relation by providing the reinforcer independent of the individual's behaviour and may reduce the individual's motivation to emit problem behaviour to obtain reinforcer because those reinforcers are freely available' (Lalli et al., 1997, p. 127).

Helping children with their homework

Quite frequently, issues related to helping children with their homework crop up in our consultation with parents. We have found that if it is not handled carefully, it has often led to a conflict between the child and the parents, and in a few cases, between parents as well. All this can have a considerable impact on the dynamics of the family and the experience can become quite fraught for all concerned.

In this section we outline some strategies that parents can employ when they have to help their children at home. Most of the advice that follows is general in nature (i.e. applies to most subjects), though we have used reading perhaps a little more frequently, as an example. Much of the advice outlined applies to infant, junior and secondary school children (see also Jenson, Sheridan, Olympia & Andrews, 1994; they have devised a package 'to train parents in effective home work practices' to help children with disabilities and behaviour disorders; Gajria & Salend, 1995, provide ideas for helping children with disabilities). In the case of secondary school children, not many parents are in a position to be able to help them with their actual homework as such, as they can when a child is in a junior school; at best, what they can do is to create an environment so that the child, without much resistance, at some stage in the evening, gets down to his work.

We mentioned above that sometimes a child's homework can be a source of conflict between parents. A good example of such a situation is the case of a six-year-old boy, Joey, with moderate learning difficulties. His parents had regular arguments about helping him with his homework. Over this issue, their arguments were so bad that it even had serious effects on their relationship. The reason for this was that his father, Edwin, felt that his mother, Jackie, did not give homework the importance it deserved but instead was far more occupied with her drinking and socialising. The other reason was that he disagreed with the way she helped him. He wanted Jackie to make him sit down, not let him fiddle around and make him work even longer than he was capable of.

There was some truth in Edwin's perspective of Jackie's dependence on drinking, socialising and being less interested in Joey's work. Equally, Edwin would not listen to Jackie that if she did not do some work on certain days it was because Joey did not bring his reading book from school. The school's policy was that if a child had finished his book, the teacher would check that the child could read it properly before changing it; until this was done, the child was not allowed to take a book home. Sometimes it took days before the teacher was able to ask the child to read to her so that his book could be changed. So on the days Jackie did not hear Joey read it was because he did not have his new book or had the same book which he had already practised at home. Jackie did not therefore want him to re-read the same book that he had already read. But Edwin felt that she should have ensured that he had brought his book home. Thus, in Edwin's view, it was Jackie's fault that he did not have his book and did not do his homework. Because of the serious differences in their relationship, they could not agree as to the best way of helping him and clarifying each other's point of view. Nor would they listen to our views, because at the time of writing this, during our clinical sessions, most of the time was spent in Jackie and Edwin attacking, blaming and criticising each other over Joey's homework and other issues.

However, in situations where there is not much disagreement between the parents over helping the child with their homework, some of the following points should reduce the tension between the child and the parents. To a certain extent, they should also help the child to be a little more cooperative when it comes to doing his homework. It is, however, acknowledged that some parents feel 'ill prepared' to be able to help their children (Kay, Fitzgerald, Parader & Mellencamp, 1994) and it is also very difficult for parents to help children who may have a history of failure and are least motivated to do their homework. It can also be difficult for parents to help children with learning difficulties because they are more easily distracted than their counterparts without any learning difficulties (Gajria & Salend, 1995) and may require specialised and/or adapted methods of providing assistance. There is some evidence which also suggests that some family variables can also have a bearing on homework outcomes; eg. educational level of parents, their socio-economic status, conditions at home (Jenson et al., 1994).

While it is true that for some parents it is difficult to help children with their homework, and some parents feel quite strongly that it is not their responsibility to help children with their homework, it is equally true that if they can manage to help, it is an important contributory factor for children's academic success (see several studies cited in: Gajria & Salend, 1995, and Jenson et al., 1994). Success and good performance can in turn have a positive effect on children's self-concept (the importance of children having positive regard about themselves has been taken up again).

1. Unlike their parents, many young children, and even adolescents, do not appreciate the importance of and need to do homework as their parents do. It would obviously please parents no end if their children valued the importance of homework as they and schools felt about it. But given their ages and stages of development, the reality is that the vast majority of the children do not. Thus there can be a significant discrepancy between the parental perception of the value of homework and their children's.

2. Whether parents like it or not, they need to accept that for a very high percentage of children, homework is just a nuisance, chore and interference with what they would really like to be doing. Because they do not like it, because they find it boring, they would do anything to avoid or delay getting down to it. If they are avoiding starting their homework, it does not mean they are being naughty. What they are doing is not dissimilar to what a large majority of adults do, including the authors of this book. If there are jobs that adults do not like doing,

they too, like their children, engage in avoidance behaviours. Parents need to understand this fully. Lack of appreciation of this on the part of the parents can lead to routine conflicts between children and their parents whenever it is homework time. Once they start seeing the reason/thinking behind why their child shows reluctance to do their homework, they are likely to become more sympathetic to the child's perspective and perhaps feel less annoyed, as well, in regard to why their child was not willingly getting down to his homework.

3. The avoidance tactics on the part of the child can become even greater if he sees his homework as difficult. If the child sees the work as hard, any pressure from parents, or nagging from them, is not going to change his perception of it, or make the child less unwilling to want to embark on it. So long as the child continues to perceive the set homework as difficult – he may or may not verbalise his feelings – it is highly probable that the child is going to continue to avoid getting down to doing it. Continued attempts to impress upon the child, either by his parents or by his teachers, that he ought to be able to do it, does not make it less difficult or encourage the child to be able to do it, or change his perception of it. Nor does it matter to the child that the majority of the children can do it. Furthermore, if the child is given the impression that he ought to be able to do it, but *he* finds it difficult, the chances are that the child is unlikely to share his feelings about the work and seek help. Clearly, if he does not get help, the problem is only going to get worse.

It is important that the child's difficulty is resolved. If it is not resolved at the right time, it can have a serious effect on his future learning, particularly if the understanding of that is crucial for the understanding of later concepts. Consider the following case. Fourteen-year-old Ian was referred to us because his teachers could not understand why he was behind with his maths and slow in understanding new concepts. At a chronological age of 14, his maths skills were at about eight-year-old level. On looking at his early records, it came to light that he had not always had difficulty with maths. In fact, when he was about eight years old, his maths ability was at a nine-year-old level. Thus, this showed that he had actually regressed. In our experience, it was not a common problem. It was, therefore, puzzling, why a boy who was doing very well with his maths up to the age of about 8–9 years, should start having serious difficulty in grasping maths concepts later on in his schooling. He was a boy of about average intellectual ability as measured on the WISC test. Nor did he have any problems with his language. Diagnostic testing of his maths skills revealed that one of his problems was that he did not understand the concept of carrying over. It became clear to us that it was the lack of understanding of this concept that was the key reason for his lack of progress in maths. Unlike the case below of the 16-year-old boy whose maths difficulties were sorted out within the term, Ian's difficulties, on the other hand, were never dealt with either at home or at school at the right time. He carried this problem unresolved until he was referred to us for an assessment and advice. Because Ian did not understand carrying over, it adversely affected his understanding of other maths concepts, particularly those that require a grasp of carrying over.

As in Ian's case, when a problem becomes long standing, with *some* children, anxiety becomes associated with that subject. Under those circumstances, the child's anxiety needs to be treated *first* before any form of intervention takes place. Invariably, if anxiety is not treated first, any educational intervention has a very limited effect. (We have dealt with this topic elsewhere; see Gupta & Gupta, 1992; also Goleman, 1996.) In circumstances such as these, it is not straightforward either for parents or teachers to be able to help such a child. A child with this type of problem needs specialist help.

On the other hand, when children's difficulties are addressed at the right time, it can save a lot of anguish for the child and a headache for the parents as well. We can recall the case of a 16-year-old boy who seriously struggled with maths for a term. Towards the end of the term he found his situation desperate and mentioned to his parents that he needed extra help with maths. The good point here is that he was able to share his difficulty with his parents because he felt confident that his difficulty would be handled sympathetically and that he would not be criticised or belittled as to why he did not understand, whereas many other children in his class could. Under these circumstances, what is important is to appreciate, to accept sympathetically and to respect the child's view of his work, though he may not overtly discuss it.

4. What can be done to make the child's homework appear either less difficult or not difficult for him? In order to do that, it is fundamental that the homework that the child has been asked to do needs to be seen by the child as within his capability and he should feel confident to be able to do it. If for some reason, the child does not, it definitely needs to be modified/adapted to bring it down to his level. For instance, the child could bring a reading book home, which is actually well above his current level of reading ability. The child's present reading age could be, say, 6.5 years. But in order to read that book, the child's reading age should be around eight years. If a child with his current reading age tries to read that book, he is likely to feel frustrated and is going to avoid reading it as well. The thing to do when

that type of situation arises is to change that book; the new book selected should have a difficulty level which is close to his present reading age, so that the child can read it without struggling excessively with it. Clearly, under these circumstances, parents need the child's class teacher's full cooperation, understanding and guidance.

Obviously, the changing of the work to a lower level needs to be handled sensitively. Whether children can or cannot, they often want to show off that they can read difficult books (or can do difficult work which the majority of their peers can do) and which do not appear 'babyish'. It is not uncommon for poor readers, when asked to pick a reading book to take home, to choose a book which is inappropriate to their current level. What is important for these children is not that they select the right kind of book but a book that looks suitably impressive to their peers and masks their limited reading ability. Alternatively, such a book could be kept for parents to read and the child to listen to the story and to look at the words; and the child could have another reading book commensurate with his current reading level. In view of what has been said above, if parents expect their child to get down to his homework with keenness and interest, it is highly unlikely that their expectations will be fulfilled and if they continue to expect this, they are likely to feel annoyed and disappointed. In other words, to avoid feelings of frustration with their children, parents' expectations of their motivation level, and interest in studies in general need to be realistic (see also 'Realistic expectations' (p. 79)).

Class teachers' help is also needed for ensuring that the child knows exactly what homework he has to do (cf. Bryan & Nelson, 1994). Sometimes children who are slow at writing, have poor spelling ability, or are generally slow, are not always able to make note of what they have to do at home. If they do not know exactly what they have to do, they are bound to be reluctant to get down to it. Thus parents need to be aware that if their child does not know exactly what homework he has to do, it is not entirely his fault and he should not be blamed for that.

Teachers' willingness to help in an understanding way can vary quite considerably, despite the emphasis over the years on parent/ teacher/school partnership. Sadly, in some schools, it is no more than lip service. Where such help from the teacher is not forthcoming, it does become very difficult for the parent to obtain the help and guidance that she needs. Should all avenues fail to elicit the child's teacher's assistance in this matter, unfortunately the only option left for the parent is to change the child's school to one which has a reputation of working closely with parents.

5. A child should never be asked to do his homework when he is in the middle of something which he is enjoying – it could be watching his favourite TV programme, or playing with his friends, or playing computer games. Under these circumstances, perhaps it is best to say that when he has finished what he is presently doing, he should start doing his homework.

6. We often recommend that parents associate a small treat with homework (we will describe this approach briefly for ready reference here; the details of the use of the rewards in general are also discussed elsewhere). For instance, let us assume that the child is very fond of some particular kind of sweets or a drink or some chocolate. It is critically important that the child really values this treat. As far as possible, this treat should not be used for any other purpose. If a child can get it too readily, it can lose its attractiveness for the child and then it is likely to be less effective. Before starting the homework, the child could be given a few sweets (assuming sweets have been selected for this purpose). When we have suggested that the child could start with one or two sweets before actually starting his work, some parents have raised two objections about this. First, they said that what about if after getting his small reward before getting down to his work, the child changes his mind and does not do any work? Secondly, should he be given any sweets when actually, he has not done any work yet? To avoid repetition, we won't address these two understandable concerns here and deal with them instead in Chapter 6 when we discuss the use of rewards as our preferred modus operandi. Then when a child has finished his work, he could be given a few more sweets.

7. Parents should stop doing the homework with the child before he gets fed up with it. If they continue to that level, there is a danger that the next time the child may not wish to come back to it and may start associating dislike with the work. It is worth remembering that a small amount of work done on a regular basis is much better than one day doing a lot and then the next few days not doing any work at all. For instance, if a child learnt three new words every day, during the course of the year he could learn almost a thousand words. Learning three new words does not take much time. Likewise, if a child did only three sums a day, imagine how many he would do in a year or two years.

8. If a child does not understand the task, the child should not be blamed for it. This can mean one of two things, or even both. First, what the child is being asked to do could be difficult for him. The other reason could be that the child needs to have the task explained differently. A child should not be blamed if he shows difficulty in understanding it. Perhaps we should also add that the parent may not intend to blame

the child, but may do so out of frustration and worries that the child is not able to master a skill appropriate for his age.

9. As far as possible, the parents should try to make the work session as enjoyable as possible, by no means an easy task!

10. Parents should try not to be critical and impatient if a child cannot do the task or if it needs to be explained a few times. If it needs to be repeated, what that often means is that the child has not mastered the task yet. Becoming impatient and getting cross would put him off from work and the next day he would be even more reluctant to return to it.

11. Consider the following concern expressed by parents of Steven: 'Problems with speech, lack of concentration. Reading for age five years. Acting like a six-year-old and in a ten-year-old body. Can't keep still.' Steven was a boy of limited ability. Unfortunately not many parents understand what impact their child's limited level of IQ has on their ability to make academic progress; that they can be slow in learning new concepts; that in order to learn something new, the child is going to require a lot of repetition and practice; that he is likely to have a limited attention span; that he could behave like a much younger child and so on. Such parents need to be advised that the way they can help such a child at home is very different compared to a typical child who is not constrained because of his limited intellectual ability or other developmental delays or disabilities. Perhaps it is worth noting here too that in such cases parents might benefit from seeking further cognitive/developmental assessment of their child to aid them in understanding the true nature and extent of his deficits.

12. Where possible, the work area needs to be quiet and distractions should be minimised. The child would find it difficult to concentrate if one of the parents decides to watch a TV programme when the child is working and he too happens to find the programme interesting. Likewise, if possible, parents should try to avoid making social phone calls, which may also be distracting for the child.

13. While parents need to be flexible, equally it is helpful if there is some time set aside when the child is going to do his homework.

14. They should also try to show genuine interest in the child's homework. If they have to spend some time with the child, it should not be viewed that it is stopping them from the other jobs that they have to do or as a general imposition.

We do not claim that the ideas that we have given above to parents over the years are exhaustive and meet each and every eventuality. However, they have been quite sufficient to address most of the concerns that parents raised in a clinical situation pertaining to issues of helping children with their homework. We acknowledge that these pointers do make a considerable demand on parents and hardly any on children. In our experience, that children who find academic work difficult are behind compared to their peers for some reason, have learning difficulties and/or have become demotivated, if parents want them to do homework without mutual aggravation, they cannot expect them to just get on with their work. They require from their parents a lot of time, effort, patience, and implementation of some of the ideas that we have described above.

Realistic expectations

When we listen to parents' concerns about their children's behaviours and their expectations, it appears to us that there is a significant mismatch between their expectations and the way children normally behave at their particular age and stage of development. It is a *very* common occurrence and we repeatedly witness that parents have unrealistic expectations from their children. In fact this mismatch between what children are capable of doing, achieving, and understanding and what parents expect from them lies at the heart of so many problems that they have with their children. We will try to give several examples to illustrate this point so that clinicians can use these and/or their own examples arising from their own experiences when they are trying to convey this point to parents.

- Sixteen-year-old Esther, who has been discussed previously, had moderate to severe learning difficulties. Her linguistic ability was extremely restricted. She could understand very simple sentences and express herself by using single words. She had an IQ of about 60 as measured on the WISC R 111. Her 50-year-old mother, a very gentle, caring, kind woman was a single parent who suffered from Myalgic Encephalomyelitis (ME) and spent most of her time at home. Obviously, her medical condition limited her in what she could and could not do. She had little support from any of her family and had very little social life. Once Esther had gone to her special school, all of her mother's day was spent staring out of the window from her sitting room. She looked forward to Esther coming home so that she could have an intelligent conversation with her. She expected that she would be able to go shopping with her, as she felt many mothers and daughters did, and Esther would share her enjoyment of shopping. She also expected from Esther that she would be able to fill her lonely and isolated life; that she would be like a normal 16-year-old girl and possibly behave like a much older girl than she actually was. Esther did not, and just was not able to meet any of these expectations; and because of her limitations, neither could she understand what was expected of her by her mother. This resulted in both mother and daughter being frustrated, irritated, and annoyed with each other. It also led to Esther beginning to present somewhat typical adolescent behaviour problems and attempting to get away from her mother by shutting herself in her bedroom. This further accentuated her mother's feelings of loneliness, dissatisfaction, and irritation with Esther. Given Esther's limitations, age, and ability, her mother's expectations of her were totally and completely unrealistic. This resulted in a hopeless vicious cycle which they were unable to break.

- It is not uncommon for parents (this often happens with mothers who have decided to stay at home and look after children) of 3–4-year-old children to expect that, when their (parents') friends have come round, their children should be able to occupy themselves without making any demands, so that they can have a chat with their friends. If the childen want their attention in these circumstances, they get annoyed with them, because they think they have been rude in interrupting them when grown-ups are talking. In this situation, mothers fail to appreciate that a typical child of this age is able to occupy himself for only short periods of time and is likely to require occasional attention. What they often end up doing is reinforcing the child's wrong patterns of behaviour by giving negative or positive attention when the child misbehaves. When that happens children learn that the only way to gain their parents' attention is by misbehaving. Mothers in this situation who expect that their child is going to occupy himself all the time their friends are there have totally unrealistic expectations. In circumstances like this, a realistic expectation would be that the child will make demands on them or want their attention; they should be prepared to offer it willingly and happily at regular intervals even *before* the child makes such a demand.

- Sometimes parents expect that their child should demonstrate his good behaviour for an unreasonably long period of time, such as a month, before he can be positively reinforced. If parents have such an expectation, the chances are that the child may not be able to fulfil it. Under these circumstances, what is likely to happen is that after trying for one or two days, the child might give up trying and then the problematic situation is likely to go back to square one.

- What is important to the child may not be important to the parents as mentioned earlier. That the child keeps his room tidy may be important for the parents and not for the child. The way a child sees his untidy room is different to the way the parent is going to see it: playing in an untidy room may not be as irritating for the child as seeing a messy room may be for the parent. Should the child be allowed to keep his room in a mess and not do anything about it? Parents do need to do something about it; but our view is that the level of tidiness expected from the child should be commensurate with his age and ability. Say a ten-year-old child, if asked to put all his games and toys away, may put some away and still leave some. In both cases, it is important for parents to recognise that to the majority of children, it does not matter what their room looks like.

- Playing on the computer now can be more important for the child than doing his homework. For parents, obviously the latter is going to be far more important than for the children. If parents expect the majority of children to attach similar significance to educational matters that they do, they are likely to be disappointed and annoyed with their children. Getting annoyed with a child is not going to teach him to value the importance of education/homework as his parents do (see also 'Helping children with their homework', p. 71).

How unrealistic expectations and criticism go hand in hand can be seen from the following letter from a father to his son. It has been taken from Carnegie (reprinted 2001) and is reproduced in its entirety. Carnegie says that this letter has been reproduced in several languages and has appeared in 'hundreds of magazines and house organs'. The title of the letter is 'Father Forgets' and it was originally written by W. Livingston Larned.

Listen, son: I am saying this as you lie asleep, one little paw crumpled under your cheek and the blond curls stickily wet on your damp forehead. I have stolen into your room alone. Just a few minutes ago, as I sat reading my paper in the library, a stifling wave of remorse swept over me. Guiltily I came to your bedside.

These are the things I was thinking, son: I had been cross to you. I scolded you as you were dressing for school because you gave your face merely a dab with a towel. I took you to task for not cleaning your shoes. I called out angrily when you threw some of your things on the floor.

At breakfast I found fault, too. You spilled things. You gulped down your food. You put your elbows on the table. You spread butter too thick on your bread. And as you started off to play and I made for my train, you turned and waved a hand and called, 'Goodbye, Daddy!' and I frowned, and said in reply, 'Hold your shoulders back!'

Then it began all over again in the late afternoon. As I came up the road I spied you, down on your knees playing marbles. There were holes in your stockings. I humiliated you before your boyfriends by marching you ahead of me to the house. Stockings were expensive – and if you had to buy them you would be more careful! . . .

. . . What has habit been doing to me? The habit of finding fault, of reprimanding – this was my reward to you for being a boy. It was not that I did not love you; *it was that I expected too much of you. I was measuring you by the yardstick of my own years* (emphasis added).

And there was much good and fine and true in your character. The little heart of you was as big as the dawn itself over the wide hills. This was shown by your spontaneous impulse to rush in and kiss me good night. Nothing else matters tonight, son. I have come to your bedside in the darkness, and I have knelt there, ashamed.

It is a feeble atonement; I know you would not understand these things if I told them to you during your waking hours. But tomorrow I will be a real daddy! I will chum with you, and suffer when you suffer, and laugh when you laugh. *I will bite my tongue when impatient words come. I will keep saying as if it were a ritual: 'He is nothing but a boy – a little boy!'* (emphasis added).

I am afraid I have visualised you as a man . . . I have asked too much, too much (emphasis added).

From what has been said above, it follows that rules and expectations should be age and ability appropriate. Unrealistic expectations lead only to frustrations and annoyance with the child, make relationships between the child and the parents unpleasant, make children feel that parents nag all the time. On the other hand, parents can feel that the child does not do as he is told, even if he is told several times; they feel that they are being disrespected and/or unappreciated. When these types of things happen children and parents can have an extremely negative view of each other.

A further consequence of unrealistic demands/expectations is that it can promote feelings of failure in children and discourage them from making further efforts. When that happens, they often feel utterly demoralised and demotivated. It can result in them thinking: 'I can't do it, so why try?' According to Coopersmith (1967), when parents have unrealistic expectations and make unrealistic demands, it can make children develop faulty self-esteem.

As we have said at the beginning of this section, many parents (including the first author) make this mistake of having unrealistic expectations from their children far too frequently and are often not even aware of it. Those parents who recognise this when their attention is drawn to it, and modify their expectations so that their expectations are commensurate with the child's overall development, find rapid improvement with a range of problems that they have with their children; they do not have to go on and on at the child. This in turn improves their quality of relationship and reduces the tension in the family interactions.

Role and development of self-concept

According to one very influential view, concept of self consists of all the ideas, perceptions and values that characterise 'I' or 'me'. It also consists of the awareness of what I am and what I can do. In other words, the self can perceive itself, which in turn influences the perception of the world, and his or her behaviour (Rogers, 1965). For example, those who perceive themselves as competent and intelligent would perceive and act upon the world quite differently from those who consider themselves as ineffectual. There is also some evidence (Place et al., 2002, and several studies cited therein) that the children who feel positive about themselves and the world around them reduce the risk of developing mental health difficulties in later life. Positive self-regard has been found to be an important 'protective' factor across all areas of risk and where children are in a variety of adverse circumstances.

How do children form a view about themselves, i.e. how is their self-concept developed (e.g. I am naughty; I am clever; I am not intelligent)? Without being deliberate about it, the emergence of self starts fairly early in our lives, and various experiences (or factors) continue enhancing, altering, maintaining, shaping (and sometimes even depressing) our self-concept. These are woven into the pattern of one's life. They may be true or false, healthy or morbid (Jersild, 1952, p. 144). In the words of Hurlock (1964), 'The child's concept of himself as a person is a mirror image of what he believes significant people in his life think of him.'

One of the most influential views concerning the development of self-concept is that of Cooley (1902) and Mead (1934). Their thesis is that the genesis of our self-conception lies in the views taken towards us by 'significant others' (e.g. parents, brothers, sisters, peers, and teachers) in our social environment. Through a process of inferring the attitudes of others towards oneself, the individual eventually incorporates what he feels to be the general views of others towards oneself (for other views as to how self-concept develops and is influenced, see review of the literature in Gupta, 1975). The following incident illustrates this quite well. The incident concerns a boy called Henry Carson who was of average ability, and was also diffident about himself and his abilities. Through sheer accident, a mouse 'triggered' a delicate point in the apparatus while his data on a college entrance examination was being scored. Consequently, he obtained a far higher score on the test which far exceeded everybody's expectations. Such a high performance led 'significant others' to revise their opinions about him. He now started to be perceived as a talented lad. As a result, the author of this incident (Lowrey, 1961, cited in Purkey, 1970) concluded by saying that Henry Carson ended up becoming one of the best-known men of his generation. The crucial conclusion from this story is to recognise that the way a child is perceived in terms of his behaviour and/or ability influences how the child sees himself. This in turn is likely to have a significant impact on the child's achievement and behaviour.

In the light of what has been said above, it appears to us that our behaviour is determined quite significantly by the way we perceive ourselves (which has been influenced by the way we are perceived by significant others), although it is difficult to quantify. The total self-concept of an individual can range from extreme negative to extreme positive. The person who sees himself as kind would try to behave in keeping with this belief. Rogers (cited in Hall & Lindsey, 1970) notes that people endeavour to maintain and enhance their self-image even if it is totally out of step with reality. Conversely, the individual whose experiences have led him to see himself as worthless will not allow in his awareness any evidence that contradicts this self-picture. If he cannot exclude it, he might reinterpret the evidence to make it congruent with his feelings of worthlessness. To illustrate this point, Hall and Lindsey (1970; see also Swann, 1996) give an interesting example. 'The person who thinks he is worthless if he receives a promotion in his work will say that "my boss felt sorry for me" or "I do not deserve it." Some people may even do poorly in the new position to prove that they are no good' (p. 533).

Since how we perceive ourselves has an important bearing on our thinking and behaviour, it is very important that parents are careful how they comment on their children's behaviours. Many parents are less inhibited in making critical comments about their children compared with making positive remarks when they are either on their own with them, or in front of their friends and relatives. Often, not being aware of the adverse consequences of their remarks, some parents frequently say such things to their children as: 'oh, he is very hyperactive all the time'; 'he is always hitting his sister'; 'he is always fighting'; 'he has no control over his temper and the slightest thing can provoke him' and so on. Unfortunately, such parents are not aware of the negative effects of their repeated critical comments on their children's self-concept and in turn the effect this can have on their behaviour.

Given that self-concept can seriously influence our behaviors, we outline below a few steps that parents could take to help their children revise their view about themselves in a positive direction.

1. They should actively look for opportunities, or try to engineer situations in such a way that they can make positive comments about them so that it helps their children revise their self-concept from negative to positive. This could be from being a naughty boy to a well behaved, kind, and considerate boy; from being a poor reader to someone who is seriously trying hard to improve their reading; from generally feeling shy in front of strangers to not feeling shy in front of them to the same extent as he used to, and so on. In this regard, it is helpful if parents avoid talking negatively about the child in front of him to their friends

and relatives. On the other hand, they could try and look for opportunities to talk positively, when he is around, in front of others.

2. Parents should be prepared to revise their own perception of their child, particularly in the positive direction, and *must* try to convey to the child that they see him differently now compared to the way they saw him previously.

3. If parents have a negative view of the child (e.g. lazy, lacking in motivation), constantly telling him does not help to change him. Parents should try to engineer situations in which the child has opportunities to act in a desirable way and is thus able to revise his self-concept.

4. Self-concepts are specific to particular domains: 'making children feel good about their athletic skills or their general worth as people does not usually have much effect on their reading skills and their feelings about being readers. Interventions that focus on self-concepts about particular domains of achievements are more likely to be effective' (Mussen et al., 1990, p. 349). In other words, being good at playing football is not going to help them to feel good about their reading ability, if they are not good at it.

Imitation in childhood/observational learning

It may seem obvious to state, but it is true that many behaviours are learnt by observing the behaviour of other people and by watching what consequences it produces for them. Imitation would therefore appear to be at the heart of observational learning. If people did not have the ability to imitate, observational learning would be unlikely to occur. Furthermore, it is important to bear in mind that, almost invariably, we do not imitate people we do not like. This is likely to apply to children as well as to adults. Imitation is a cognitive ability and a deficit in the child's ability to imitate would have an impact on his overall intellectual development. In other words, imitation plays a crucial role in children's acquiring new skills and behaviours from opportunities naturally available to them (Flavell, 1970a; see Mussen et al., 1990 and several studies cited therein; Rogers, Hepburn, Stackhouse & Wehner, 2003). Some ability to imitate is present even in new-born babies and develops quite considerably by the time a child is two years of age (Hanna & Meltzoff, 1993; Meltzoff & Moore, 1989). It would also seem that imitation skills of toddlers with developmental disorders including autism are impaired compared to normal developing children (see Rogers et al., 2003). Thus imitation is an important developmental skill and we continue to learn by imitation even when we are older.

Sometimes parents wonder why children are selective in what they imitate. There are a few hypotheses as to whether the child will or will not imitate what they have observed. In the act of imitation, a number of processes are implicated and imitation serves different functions at different stages of the child's development. For this reason, the motivation to imitate at two years of age will be different from that at age six or at 15. Children are likely to imitate if it does not appear too difficult to copy. In one experiment, many two-year-old children stopped playing, protested, clung to their mother, and cried subsequent to seeing the experimenter display actions that were difficult for them to understand or remember well (Kagan, 1981). On the other hand, children did not show any distress when the actions that were shown to them were easy to imitate.

All this would suggest that learning by imitation is not as simple as some parents tend to think: for example, when they believe that their two-year-old child has started imitating his ten-year-old brother's defiant behaviour – an observation some parents often make.

Modelling

Learning through modelling is based on the notable work of Bandura (1977a); unlike Skinner, he is of the opinion that some learning can take place without any reinforcement. Highlighting the importance of learning by imitation/observation, Bandura (1977b) says: 'most human behaviour is learned observationally through modelling: from observing others one forms an idea of how new behaviours are performed, and on later occasions this coded information serves as a guide for action' (p. 22). By observing other people's behaviour, we can model our behaviours on theirs. Trent (2000) compares it with the

'monkey see, monkey do' assumption where a person (or animal) watches another and performs in a similar way. This principle of modelling or observational learning was used in a no smoking campaign some years ago. First, a father was seen washing his car and his young son was washing the tyre with him. The father then went on to mow the lawn and his son copied his father's behaviour by pushing a toy lawn mower. Then the advertisement showed father lighting a cigarette and the son reaching for the packet. (Trent, 2000; for details of the processes inherent in modelling see Bandura, 1977a)

Bandura's theory of modelling/observational learning has generated a considerable body of research, which provides some empirical support to his theory. For instance, in a sample of 30 toddlers, Gerull & Rapee (2002) studied the influence of parental modelling on the acquisition of fear and avoidance. The results showed that these toddlers exhibited expressions of greater fear and avoidance of the stimuli (a rubber snake and a spider were used as stimuli) following negative reactions from their mothers. The authors concluded that: 'The strong observational learning results are consistent with views that modelling constitutes a mechanism by which fear may be acquired early in life' (Gerull & Rapee, 2002, p. 279). A similar view is expressed by Wood et al. (2003) who, following a review of some of the studies concerning parental modelling of anxious behaviours, stated: 'Parents who model poor coping strategies, such as catastrophising and avoidance, are more likely to have children who lack the ability to regulate fear and anxiety effectively' (p. 142). Wood et al. also provide some evidence about the converse situation; i.e., children who do not witness much anxious behaviour in their parents tend to be less anxious themselves.

Alluding to several earlier studies, Mussen et al. (1990) point out that modelling is an effective strategy for teaching children pro-social behaviours, such as altruism. Mussen et al. also observe that personal histories of exceptionally altruistic individuals show the contribution of their parental modelling and identification in their children's acquiring of such behaviours.

Given that modelling plays quite a crucial role in our learning process, it is therefore imperative that parents set a good example for children; if they do not, their own behaviours are likely to be copied as the following examples show. There was often a 'battle' between a 16-year-old boy with moderate learning difficulties and with William's Syndrome and his stepdad because of the boy playing music very loud. Michael used to ask how come his father gets cross with him if he thought his music was loud when his father keeps the volume of his TV very loud.

One of the concerns of a nine-year-old intelligent child's mother was that her son was quite violent towards her; when he could not get his own way, he often used to hit his mother. During the interview session, when Benjamin was asked why he hit his mother, he responded by saying that she hit him when she was angry. So he hit her when he was angry, or when he felt that she was being unfair. During the session, it was explained to Mum why it was important to set a good example. In the light of this discussion, it was agreed that Mum should not use hitting as a sanction. Benjamin agreed too that if his mother did not hit him, he would not hit her. When Benjamin's mother was seen again, she reported that neither of them had hit each other since they were last seen. (It needs to be added that normally behaviours do not change as rapidly as this brief case history shows.)

It therefore follows that a child should be treated as the parents like to be treated themselves. A 15-year-old boy said to us that when his parents are asleep, if he is a little bit noisy, he gets shouted at. On the other hand, when he is asleep, his parents do not care how much noise they make.

The issue of modelling can be summed up by an ancient Indian folklore tale. In appreciating this story, a Western reader needs to bear in mind that this story has been translated from an Indian language. In so doing, it may have lost some nuances. This story dates back many centuries ago when there was no transport and people travelled by foot irrespective of the distances involved. The tale goes that there was a middle-aged woman and she had a young son who suffered from some kind of skin disorder. This mother had heard from an acquaintance in the village that there was a sage who lived about 40 miles away from where she lived, and he had the knowledge, skill and charisma to cure her son. One day she decided to take her son to this wise man. Thus, her young son and this woman walked all the way to see this man. It took them quite a few days to walk this distance. When they saw him, this sage looked carefully at this young man's skin disorder. After he had examined him, he reflected for some time and then said to this mother: 'Come back and see me after a month. I am not ready yet to recommend what your son should do.' The poor woman and her son walked back all the way again.

After a month they went and saw this man again. The sage said the same thing as he had said the first time, i.e. 'I am not quite ready to recommend any treatment yet; come back after a month'. They went back after a month again, as the mother was so desperate to have her son cured. This sage said the same thing yet again. This happened quite a few times. Eventually, on the woman's sixth visit, the wise man said that this time he was ready to advise her and her son as to what should be done to cure his skin disorder. He calmly said to them that he should not eat anything with sugar in it. The mother felt somewhat cross inside with this man but still humbly and respectfully asked him: 'Why could not you tell me the first time I came? Surely you could have told me then. I am sure you knew about this even then. My son and I have put ourselves to so much inconvenience during all these months by having to keep coming every month.' The sage did not feel offended that this woman was questioning him but very serenely said to them that he could not advise them during their previous visits because at that time, he too ate a lot of things which had sugar in them. If he had advised them when he ate sugary things himself, it would not have had any effect on her son. It took him all that time to stop eating sugary things himself and he did not wish to give this advice while he was eating sweet things. Now that he had stopped eating sugar himself, he could advise with confidence and he was sure that her son would listen to him and do what he was told to do!

Although just folklore, the message is quite clear and appears to be psychologically sound. Children are less likely to pay attention to what parents say if they think/perceive that their parents engage in similar behaviours themselves; for instance, parents should not expect their children not to swear if they swear themselves in front of them. Likewise, they should not expect them not to fly off the handle, if that's what they do themselves. If parents want their children to learn not to defend their position when they are wrong, they need to set a good example themselves. They should be open, frank, and apologetic, when they have been wrong. In time, children will learn to acknowledge and accept that they are wrong, when the parents think their children have erred. It would be helpful if they remember, what has been rightly said above: 'monkey see, monkey do'!

5

IMPORTANT GENERAL POINTERS FOR PARENTS

In this chapter, we turn our attention to some other pointers, which we have called general pointers. These pointers, on the whole, are not as detailed as the ones that have been described in the previous chapter. Possibly the main reason for this is that those pointers have required elaborate treatment compared to the ones outlined here. It is perhaps also true to say that they have cropped up more frequently in our clinical work than those outlined here. The separation of these pointers into separate chapters, however, is largely arbitrary. The essential preliminaries outlined in the previous chapter apply equally to the following pointers.

1. Sometimes there is a considerable divergence between the child's perception of a situation and that of the parents. Parents may find that the child's teacher is perfectly reasonable and fair. Their perception is based on the way the teacher presents himself when parents see him when it is parents' evening. On the other hand, the child finds the teacher unfair and unhelpful. When such a situation arises, there would be a tendency on the part of the parents to try and convince the child that his teacher is perfectly all right. If the child's views are well entrenched based on *his* experience and perception, parents may decide that even though they are older, more experienced and better judges of character they are not likely to help revise the child's views about the teacher. However, if the child tries at any time to express his unhappiness about his teacher, it is not uncommon for many parents to launch into trying to convince the child, contrary to the emotions that the child is trying to express. Consider the following three examples as well, which have been taken from Faber & Mazlish (2001), and which further illustrate how parents quite frequently reject when a child tries to express an opinion over some issue.

Example 1
Child: I'm tired.
Parent: You couldn't be tired.
Child (*saying louder*):   But I'm tired.
Parent: You're not tired. You're just a little sleepy. Get dressed.

Example 2
Child: It's hot in here.
Parent: It's cold. Keep your sweater on.
Child: No, I'm hot.
Parent: I said, 'Keep your sweater on.'
Child: No, I'm hot.

Example 3
Child: That TV show was boring.
Parent: No it was not. It was interesting.
Child: It was stupid.
Parent: It was educational.
Child: It stunk.
Parent: Don't talk that way.

When this happens repeatedly, not only may such disagreements lead to arguments, but they may also result in poor communication between the child and parents. Furthermore, a child may start to believe that his parents do not listen to and believe him. Yet another drawback if parents frequently reject the child's perception of the events is that they are unwittingly conveying to the child that his feelings, views, and understanding of the situation are worthless which can be detrimental to his self-worth. Under these circumstances, it is best to accept, and if possible, respect, how the child feels about the situation, irrespective of how the parents think about it. Continually telling the child is not going to convince him that his parents are right and that he needs to revise his opinion about the teacher, or for that matter, whenever a divergence of views arises.

2. Parents need to take active steps to redress the situation, if they often hear their child saying to them (or if parents sense that their child feels) that they are being unfair to him, although they may not think that way. If a child continues to harbour these feelings against his parents, he is likely to develop negative feelings against them and this can lead to breakdown of the relationship between child and parents. Once this begins to happen, parents can begin to lose control over their child.

3. It helps the situation if parents try to see the problem from the child's point of view as well. Sometimes parents do not know how the child

sees the problem. This could be because the child had not told them; or it had not occurred to them that there could be a divergence between the way they saw the problem and the way their children might perceive it; or, they might even have asked the child but he still had not told them, thinking perhaps that even if he did tell them, nothing was likely to happen. A good example of such a case was that of 15-year-old Lucy. She was referred to us for problems such as depression, keeping distant from parents and being somewhat aggressive towards them. When seen, she said that *one* of the reasons for her problems was that her parents did not listen to her and whenever she tried to say anything to them she was always interrupted. Her parents had never realised that this is what they had inadvertently been doing over the years and how much unhappiness this had caused to Lucy. Once their attention was drawn to it, without any defence they acknowledged it and stopped doing it. Surprisingly, Lucy's problems, following one consultation session, improved very significantly.

Also, there is a small minority of parents who refuse to see problems from the child's standpoint and steadfastly continue to believe that the cause of the problem lies with the child. This can be briefly illustrated by alluding to the case of Josh, which we have mentioned elsewhere in the book as well. His parents, even after 11 months of therapeutic intervention, still refused to *see* their child's behaviour problems from his perspective. Consequently, the family dynamics never improved.

4. Parents should try and not labour a point – for instance, by saying to the child frequently that he should read every day because it is good for him. True, it is good for the child, but repeatedly telling him is neither going to convince him nor going to help him acquire new patterns of behaviours that parents would like their child to learn. If anything, if a child hears his parents wishing him to do something repeatedly, he may put up a barrier and may start doing just the opposite. We can recall the case of a 13-year-old girl whose parents often criticised her for talking with a Birmingham accent; her parents felt that it made her sound very common. The consequence of her parents repeatedly telling her was that she started talking with an exaggerated Birmingham accent (see Chapter 6 for strategies that can be used to modify children's behaviours).

5. Do not allow children's behaviours to drive a wedge between the parents' relationship. Children's behaviours and interactions, and demands on parents and the way they (parents) together, and separately, handle them can have a deleterious effect on the parents' relationships with each other. Many children, of almost all ages, are chiefly concerned to satisfy their own desires. They will not appreci-

ate that in the long run, should the parents' relationship deteriorate, it will not be helpful to the child. If parents sense this happening, they should set aside some time, twice a week, if possible, when they can go over these issues, and try to prevent it from happening before the parents' relationship significantly deteriorates. In one case, it resulted in parents having to live separately.

6. Parents often try and ask a child why he misbehaved. Invariably they never get a satisfactory response. Tracey said that she often questioned her daughter, Sam, about why she attempted to hurt herself when she was angry with her mother. The only answer she got from Sam was that she did not know. It is possible that the child does not know the answer because it is a learnt response and each time he is in that kind of situation, he comes up with the habitual response. Thus it is often true that the child genuinely does not know why he misbehaved. Sometimes this kind of question is asked from a very young child who does not have the intellectual and verbal ability to explain.

7. It makes a child's behaviour worse if parents disagree with their management. They need to offer a united front. It does not mean that they need to be carbon copies of each other. Not only the parents, but if other caregivers are also involved with whom the child spends a considerable amount of time, they should all try and work the same way. Significantly different management styles between the parents are not helpful to the child. Children will exploit warring parents. Conflicting messages from parents and other carers are likely to make bad behaviours worse. For instance, one parent does not say 'no' unnecessarily; the other parent thinks that if you say 'yes' to your child's demands, even when you can, this is like giving in. Thus, in order to keep the peace between parents, one less dominant parent starts saying 'no' just to please the other partner, even though she does not agree with it.

8. Parents need to be consistent over time. It is no good being rewarding today and being punitive and ignoring good behaviour the next day. Such inconsistency is not going to help bring desirable changes in the child's behaviour.

9. Parents need to set aside some time so that they can discuss how their behaviour management strategies are working. Obviously, they need to carry on with what works and do less of what does not. If they know shouting does not make child behave, there is little point in carrying on with it. This means they need to sit back and examine their parenting style.

10. Undesirable behaviours should not be rewarded by unwittingly giving in or paying attention to the child when he is misbehaving.

11. Sometimes parents get cross with the child because he has not done what he has been asked to do. The reality is that the child may not have understood what he had been asked to do in the first place. This happens more often when children have moderate learning difficulties and their linguistic ability could be impaired as well. Parents often have not fully grasped the implications of this when they give complex commands to the child.

12. Act firmly and promptly to ensure that your rules are adhered to by your child. It is pointless asking a child to do something and not making sure that he does it. If parents are not going to follow through with their command, it is best not to give the command. We would also suggest that if they are not following through with their command, and the parent does not notice, it probably is unnecessary and they can do without it. This was evident in the clinic situation in the case of six-year-old Luke who came to see us with his mother. Luke presented a number of behaviour problems both at home and at school. The school could not cope with him in the class situation. The only way they could keep him in school was by offering him 1:1 help. At home, he threw things when he could not have his own way; attacked his mother, brothers and sister, according to his mother, without any provocation. In the clinic situation, where he was a law unto himself, we have not seen many children behaving as inappropriately as Luke did. We noticed how his mother was telling him not to do certain things but not ensuring that he followed through what she asked him not to do.

Towards the end of our session, he started to mess around with the drawer of the first author's desk. Several times he tried to move my foot with his hands, so that he could open the drawer. I put my foot firmly against it to ensure that he was not able to open it. Luke got the non-verbal message that no matter what he did, he was not going to be allowed to open the drawer. Once he got the message, he stopped persevering and without any temper or fuss moved himself away from that situation.

13. Children must feel that they are listened to and that their views are valued. If they make a good point, be prepared to accept it gracefully and praise the child for making such a good point. It needs to be conveyed that he has made a good point. Parents should not think that because they are older, therefore, only they have the monopoly on making sensible suggestions. Children too can and should be encouraged to do so. If it involved changes in parents' behaviour or thinking, not only should they do that but they should also ensure that the child sees that they have incorporated the child's suggestion in their own repertoire. By so doing parents are setting a good example to the child. The child is likely to show less resistance in adopting the

parents' ideas, as well, when they see that their ideas are valued and adopted by their parents.

14. It is an understandable action on the part of the parents to leave the child to occupy himself with an activity so that they can get on with the jobs they have to do. The danger with this approach is that the child is unlikely to engage with what he is doing without making any demands on the parent. If the parent starts paying attention when the child misbehaves, then what they are doing is unwittingly reinforcing wrong patterns of behaviour. This is helping the child to learn that if they behave badly, they will get their parents' attention. In order to ensure that the child continues to occupy himself, the best thing is occasionally to praise the child, comment about him behaving nicely as he is so well occupied, and even join him in his play. After the parent has paid some attention for a while, they can get back and carry on with whatever they were doing previously. The mindset of many parents is that if they are cleaning or cooking they cannot stop unless they have finished what they are doing. Authors take the view that many of the jobs parents do is not like doing heart surgery or brain surgery, where a pause could cause serious damage to the patients. In the home situation, many jobs parents have to do can be stopped, if need be. It takes far less time to help maintain good behaviour rather than having to attend when the child has started to misbehave. Whenever parents' attention has been drawn to it, they have immediately appreciated this logic. More importantly, the parent under those circumstances is also teaching the child that bad behaviour earns him parents' attention. This often increases the frequency of bad behaviours.

15. There is a danger that parents can begin to take their children's improvement for granted. They keep changing the goalposts and thus continue to criticise and be dissatisfied with whatever improvement the child has shown in his behaviour.

16. Also there are situations when parents have seen some improvement but attribute it to the child's ulterior motives. Fifteen-year-old Mark's father reported some improvement in his confrontational behaviour in the last few weeks. Father's interpretation was that he was trying to be nice because he was after something. It is better to err on the side of reinforcing, even if parents suspect that there are some other reasons for exhibiting that kind of behaviour.

17. Whenever possible parents should not use empty threats which they cannot carry through. On the way to school, a parent might say to the child that if he did not hold her hand properly, he would not get sweets after the school. After school the parent has forgotten what was said in the morning and the child still gets the sweets in spite of

the fact that he did not do what he was asked to do. The parent in anger may say to the child that he is not allowed to watch the cartoons on TV for his misdemeanour. Then she does not follow it through when the child puts cartoons on the TV. When this is repeatedly done, the children get used to it and take no notice of the threats when they are given. It can result in parents having to give more and more serious threats. It reaches a point that no matter how serious a threat they use, they seem to have little effect in controlling the child's behaviour. When that happens it can make parents look helpless, embarrassed, and they do not know just what to do to get compliance from their children. The child can appear to be totally in charge of the situation – just the opposite to what parents wanted and hoped that the threat would produce.

The case of a six-year-old adopted child provides a good example of a parent using quite a serious empty threat following her bad behaviour. Ruby, for her age, was very stubborn and difficult to manage at home and her adoptive mother, Mrs F, was completely at her wits' end over her. Ruby's behaviour in school was regarded as satisfactory. Ruby had a four-year-old brother who also lived with her. Along with Ruby, he too was adopted by Mrs F. Mrs F said that she had 'tried everything' but somehow nothing worked with her. One day, following Ruby's 'seriously naughty behaviour', in complete desperation she threatened that she would get rid of Ruby by giving her to another family. Following this, Mrs F told Ruby to go upstairs and pack up and come down and then she would take her to the other family. Without the show of any emotions, Ruby went upstairs, packed what she could, and came down ready to be taken to another family. It did worry Mrs F that her threat, so far, was having little effect on her. Mrs F felt that she had to go through with her threat. She took Ruby out, drove her round for some time, hoping that she might show some emotions and regret. Ruby exhibited neither. At last, Mrs F took Ruby to a quiet place and told her to get out of the car and said that she was going to be picked up by the other family from there. Ruby quietly got out of the car and waved her adoptive mother goodbye and Mrs F drove off for fifty or so yards. Seeing that all this had no effect, at least outwardly, Mrs F had no choice but to drive back to her to pick her up to take her home. This incident, at least apparently, had a more devastating effect on Mrs F than on Ruby, but also may have sent a damaging message to Ruby that her adoptive mother wished to give her away.

18. A child is highly unlikely to enter into any sensible discussion shortly after – and for some time after – there has been any disagreement or argument between the child and the parents. At that time, rightly or

wrongly, the child would feel that he was right and his parents were wrong. Under these circumstances, he is not going to listen to the parents. If parents persist in their efforts to ask the child why he behaved the way he did, a possible outcome of this is that the child might become accustomed to his parents' habit of going on and on. Under these circumstances, the child is likely to switch off. The danger is that he may develop a habit of not listening to his parents even when he is not upset.

In many ways the child's behaviour is not too dissimilar from grown-ups when they are upset or feel aggrieved. Under those circumstances, grown-ups are not likely to enter into any sane discussion with the other party; they are unlikely to view the situation objectively and are likely to blame the other person for whatever has happened. It is best, in circumstances like this, to leave the issue until tempers on both sides have calmed down and there is some willingness to sort out the problem or discuss the matter.

19. Another situation where it is very tempting for parents to 'lecture' their children is when, for instance, they are together either for the family meal or when they are going out together. This type of 'lecture' can come totally out of the blue. If a child does not eat much fruit the parents may launch into an explanation that he should eat more fruit; or if he does not read much they may start telling the child the importance of reading; or the lecture could be on good manners. It is not difficult to understand why parents want their children to do better and hence their reason for 'lecturing'. We think the trouble is that more often than not the child has heard those explanations before. When they hear parents launching into this, children are likely to switch off or change the topic and eventually avoid being with parents because they may form a view that whenever they are with their parents, they have to endure their 'lectures'.

20. Lectures do have their place and time. Parents have to teach a lot of things to their children. They need to be aware that their lectures do not need to be often repeated and long-winded, and should be avoided when the child wants to be with them. Otherwise, the child is unlikely to want to be around them. It is worth reminding parents that the less time a child spends with them, the fewer opportunities he has of observing their behaviours and hopefully imbibing them and incorporating them into his own behaviours.

21. Parents often do a lot of things for their children. A large majority of them have to be done. These include cooking, washing, buying presents for various occasions, entertaining his friends, fetching and taking him from school, taking him to the doctor when he is unwell, to name a few. There is no doubt that all this is tiring, demanding,

stressful, and expensive for the parents. Often, in trying to meet the child's demands, there is not much time and energy left for them.

Over the years, the child begins to think that these are parents' jobs and not much more than that. The problem begins to arise when parents think that the child ought to show some appreciation of what they do for him and this should be manifested in his behaviour. In other words, the child ought to do what he is asked to do and generally show good behaviour. When they see that not happening, they can begin to feel hurt, disappointed, and annoyed and infer that the child does not show any appreciation for all the things that they do for him. The mother of an eight-year-old boy said to us that she and Gordon's father took him and his brother out for the day, and shortly after they came back, he started to misbehave. Gordon's parents' expectation was that they had spent a lot of time and money on him and his brother, and he should show some appreciation at least for a few days by displaying good behaviour. It is an unsavoury fact for parents that this is not likely to happen. Once they come back, the child's behaviour is going to be determined by how they interact with him. Once parents begin to realise that the child is unlikely to show any feelings of gratitude and good behaviour because of all they do for him, then this is likely to reduce their bitterness and frustration with the child.

22. If parents want any respect and wish to build a good relationship with their children from childhood through to adolescence, it is very important that they do things for them which they particularly like and value. (As has already been said above, a lot of the day-to-day things that are done for them they just take for granted.) For instance, if the parent knows that their child likes any particular kind of food, they should produce it as a surprise. When the child is not expecting it, offer to play with him in a way that the child likes, even if it may not be particularly great fun for the parent. When parents do things like this on a regular basis that help the child develop warm and affectionate feelings for his parents, he is likely to listen and do more things for his parents than when he has negative feelings.

23. When things go wrong in life and do not turn out as planned, parents generally feel frustrated, disappointed and easily irritable. When they are feeling that way, they unwittingly take out their frustrations on their children, particularly if they find they do not toe the line straight-away. Parents need to recognise that children are not able to read parents' minds; nor would they appreciate to the same extent as parents the impact those frustrations and disappointments are having on them. Under these circumstances, should parents get cross with

their children, children are likely to consider their parents' behaviour as unreasonable and unfair. When children see that happen repeatedly, it is not conducive to a good relationship between children and parents.

24. Although not always easy, particularly when parents are feeling angry with their child, humour sometimes can diffuse the situation and stop it from escalating.

25. Children's privacy should be respected. For instance, parents should not assume that they have a right just to barge into their child's room without knocking or alerting the child about it. In turn, children should also learn to respect their parents' privacy (see 'Modelling', p. 86).

26. Parents should avoid saying 'I told you so'. Little purpose would be served from labouring to prove that the child was wrong. If parents frequently do this, the chances are that the child would feel embarrassed and might use defence mechanisms to prove that he was not wrong. Because of this, he may not learn what parents want him to learn. Probably the best thing is that the child is made aware that they know that he was wrong. This may have a more desired effect.

27. Children should be given the feeling that parents are happy to accept their ideas, even if it means doing things different to the way you have done them in the past. If it turns out to be a better idea, have an open mind and be willing to say so to the child.

28. Children's worries or anxieties, no matter how trivial, should not be underestimated. What may seem trivial to the parent may be very important for the child and may have considerable effect on his behaviour. A head teacher of a junior school once reported how a parent went to see him and said that her six-year-old daughter had started to show signs of not wanting to come to school. There was no apparent reason for this. After spending a lot of time, it came to light that about a month earlier, the children had their furniture changed during their lunch hour. They now had higher tables and each child did not have the right size chair. This girl found that her chair in relation to the table was low for her and she could not eat properly. Once they found out that that was the reason, she was given a chair of the right size. With that, the girl became the usual happy little girl that she used to be. Thus a grown-up may feel that it was a trivial thing to stop her from wanting to go to school. Further, they may wonder why she did not go and tell the teacher about this, in which case the problem would have been resolved. That is not the point being made here. It is simply that something trivial may be perceived as big by the child and it needs to be handled sensitively and not just dismissed. If it is not given due importance, it is also conceivable that in the future the

child may feel reluctant to share his anxiety with his parents. Conversely, when a child's concerns are handled sensitively, he is likely to have increased respect for his parents for showing concern and understanding for his worries and anxieties.

29. Parents need to congratulate and reward themselves when, as a result of their own time and perseverance, they have succeeded in improving their child's behaviour. Six-year-old Leighana's stepdad came and told us that his stepdaughter's soiling had improved quite considerably compared with what she used to be like. He started attributing her improvement to her friends who came to play with her, and also to her becoming more aware that if she smelt, other children would laugh at her. In outlining all these reasons, he did not see the important role that he played in helping his stepdaughter to overcome her problem. Parents' attention needs to be drawn to what they had achieved as, obviously, it is positively reinforcing for them and this would help them to persevere in their attempts to modify their children's behaviours.

30. Apart from the reconstituted families, parents are wholly responsible for bringing their children into this world. Thus, unconsciously, they should not resent having to do things for their children or when they make demands on their parents. Children can give parents a lot of pleasure, as they can give a lot of grief.

It would clearly be obvious to clinicians that one does not need to use all the pointers with each and every family who are seen by them. Different pointers are helpful in different situations. As well as using the appropriate pointers, we also use an adapted version of behaviour modification, the details of which have been outlined in the next chapter.

6

AN ADAPTED, ACCEPTABLE, AND EFFECTIVE BEHAVIOUR MODIFICATION APPROACH

INTRODUCTION

Perhaps, as a result of the current emphasis on evidence-based practice, literature on empirically supported therapies is growing. Notwithstanding this, it is ironical – though understandable – that 'the treatment approaches with the best empirical support are rarely used in typical clinical practice' (Coxhead & Gupta, 1989; Gupta & Parry-Gupta, 2003; Connor-Smith & Weisz, 2003). This is not new. In the early 1980s, following their survey, Coxhead and Gupta (1989) highlighted that practising educational psychologists did not use behaviour modification in its traditional format (for details of such an approach, see Gelfand & Hartmann, 1975). This is in spite of the fact that traditional behaviour modification has an enviable track record for its effectiveness in various settings. Their survey showed that most practising educational psychologists (EPs) had little or no commitment to the traditional view of behaviour modification (i.e. the way the experimental evidence would suggest that behaviour modification should be used). The survey also showed that few EPs believed that traditional behaviour modification should be implemented without any adaptation. An interesting, and somewhat unexpected finding was that a vast majority of the respondents held rather unfavourable attitudes towards the traditional form of behaviour modification, although more experienced EPs were less antagonistic. It is acknowledged that the survey we have referred to is somewhat dated. However, our more recent experience of working in different clinics in the last ten years would suggest that, if we were to repeat this survey, we would be likely to obtain similar results. We will even go as far as saying that, in our considerable experience of working in different setups, we have never come across any psychologist using traditional forms of behaviour modification.

As well as referring to some of the published literature, Gupta and Coxhead (1990) outlined some of the reasons why in clinical settings, or for that matter in schools, behaviour modification in its traditional format is difficult to implement. For instance, Hyman and Lally (1982) observed that traditional behaviour modification does not adequately deal with the question of generalisability, its poor reliability, and its unsatisfactory experimental design. Kazdin (1980) has criticised traditional behaviour modification for lack of 'social' validation. According to Bolton et al. (2003; see also the studies cited therein): 'While intervention aimed at modifying parenting skills is important, purely behavioural models of treatment may neglect emotional and cognitive features of parent–child interaction' (p. 242). Tharp and Wetzel (1969), drawing on their experience of using behaviour modification in 'natural settings', concluded as follows:

> In the natural environment, however, things do not work out with such simplicity. Adequate reinforcers are not always available, either for the target or mediators. Logistical problems are sometimes insurmountable. Indeed, few cases did not include at least one form of these resistances, most resisted in several ways . . . The point made here is that these resistances cannot be assumed unique to any one case. They represent technical difficulties which must be faced by anyone who chooses to attempt behaviour modification in the natural environment. Thus some resistances help us to perceive the limitations on the advisability of behaviour modification in the natural environment. (pp. 126–7)

Furthermore, it seems totally unreasonable – and perhaps would be unacceptable – to many parents who have waited sometimes as long as three months to a year to be seen for the first time (depending upon the waiting list of a clinic), for the clinician to send them away to collect the baseline data so that comparisons can be made on whether any change in the child's behaviour can be attributed to the therapeutic input. It also seems unreasonable and unrealistic to make demands of at least a good number of parents that are seen at CAMHS because of their complex lifestyles, as collecting data before any intervention can be implemented would just be an additional burden for them.

The difficulties that have been outlined in implementing behaviour modification in its traditional format are not just peculiar to behaviour modification only, but to other therapies, as well, which have empirical support. In fact, Kazdin (2002) notes that 'The ways in which psychotherapy is studied depart considerably from how the treatment is implemented in clinic practice' (p. 54). Kazdin goes on to explain why this is the case and among other differences, draws attention to the differences in the clinical population and the populations employed in the research designs (see also Connor-Smith & Weisz, 2003; Harrington, Cartwright-Hatton & Stein, 2002; Hotopf, Churchill & Lewis, 1999; Wolpert, 2002). However, from the foregoing discussion, it should not be inferred that we are advocating that the available evidence should not form the basis of one's clinical judgement or one's decision-making; that one should be somewhat cavalier in using empirically supported evidence in one's clinical practice. On the contrary, in this matter, our position is very much in line with the British Psychological Society (Wolpert, 2002). According to the BPS, our clinical practice should be an integration of our clinical expertise 'and the best available external evidence from systematic research in order to reach decisions about client care' (Wolpert, 2002, p. 5).

Given that no matter how efficacious and empirically sound a therapeutic approach may be, if, in the clinic situation, it appears impractical to clinicians and unacceptable to the recipients (who may be families or teachers), it is highly unlikely that it is going to be implemented and adhered to in the way it was developed or intended (cf. Kazdin & Wassell, 2000a). Kazdin et al. (1997) have also shown that if a treatment plan is perceived by parents as demanding and of little relevance to the child's problems, it can influence family's dropout rate from the treatment programme.

It is in the light of some of these considerations that over the years we have adapted and modified behaviour modification so that families do not put up barriers against it. By adapting it, we feel that what we have done is, we are using a very efficacious, exceedingly well-researched therapeutic approach, but we are using it flexibly and have tailored it to the needs of our families (cf. Connor-Smith & Weisz, 2003). Also, this approach incorporates our thinking and experience which underpin some of our pointers which have been detailed in the previous pages.

ADAPTED AND ACCEPTABLE BEHAVIOUR MODIFICATION APPROACH

In earlier pages, in the form of brief case studies, we have referred to a whole range of behaviour problems that clinicians often come across in a clinic situation. Our therapeutic approach that we have used in all those cases now follows. In certain cases, a small change, without having to implement all aspects of our approach, can set off a virtuous cycle, i.e. it leads to a significant improvement in the child's behaviours and/or interactions between the child and his parents. Again, we have referred to this earlier on as well.

It is acknowledged that we do not have empirically sound data to provide a backup for our approach and the claims that we have made about its efficacy are based on our experience of using it. This approach has evolved over the years, following our experience of using it and not by following a conscious process trying to develop a therapeutic approach per se. With this approach, we have been more concerned by subjectively looking at its effectiveness rather than attempting to study how it works. Given that so many factors could be impinging which help in bringing about change, it is not always realistic and practical to be able to attribute that change to the therapeutic process that has been used; it is also virtually impossible to be able to say with any certainty how it has worked (cf. Kazdin & Nock, 2003), although scientifically speaking, it may be highly desirable.

Some Assumptions that Underlie Our Approach

In our approach to behaviour modification, there are some common assumptions which stem from Brief Solution Focused Therapy (Lethem, 2002). Some of them are:

1. Understanding the underlying causes of the problem is helpful but not necessarily a step towards resolution of the problem.
2. Notwithstanding the complexity of the problem, it is perfectly conceivable that the parents are doing certain things which are helpful in dealing with the child's problem.
3. Obviously, what is 'helpful' needs to be identified and when parents come to see a clinician they may not be aware of that.
4. Except in a minority of cases, the majority of the problems do not have underlying pathologies.

As well as incorporating the above assumptions into our system, there are some other significant and important variables that are *sine qua non* to our approach. The first of them is the great importance that we give to parents' well-being (a topic which we have addressed in the previous pages as well, although from a somewhat different standpoint): our rationale for doing that follows next.

Using Additional Variables in Our Approach

Importance of parental well-being

At the very start of this book, we stated that raising children is stressful; bringing up children who have some kind of problems – e.g. physical, emotional, behavioural, learning – is even more stressful. On this matter, our views have been considerably shaped by our experience of working with families we see in the clinic situation and the effect it can have on their mental well-being and then the way they start seeing the problems. For instance, three-year-old Jamie was perceived by his mother as very hyperactive, unable to concentrate, and defiant, and she was convinced that he had ADHD. His nursery, which he attended on three mornings a week, had absolutely no concern about his behaviour, or his ability to concentrate. When he was taken to the referrer, his family doctor, he saw no problems with Jamie's behaviour. In the clinic situation, we saw him twice. During that time, we saw no symptoms which are commonly associated with ADHD. We would describe the behaviour that we saw as exemplary. Unfortunately, what had been happening in this situation was that his mother suffered from depression. Because she felt 'drained' all the time, even his perfectly normal behaviour seemed abnormal to her. Then she passed this information to her parents who were also involved in his upbringing. Then they started perceiving him as having a number of behaviour problems, as well.

Thus, in our version of behaviour modification, parental mental or physical state, and their general circumstances are taken into account before we introduce our adapted version of behaviour modification. We feel that unless parents are up to it themselves, they are not able to cope with the extra demands made by the traditional behaviour modification or any approach which does not take into account parental circumstances and the cognitive–affective aspects of parenting (Bugental & Johnston, 2000; Kazdin & Whitley, 2003).

The following case study is one of the examples of the way we try to address parental stress and how dealing with their stress is an integral part of our approach. A 20-year-old single mother with a three-year-old autistic son (a case study which has been mentioned in the previous pages as well) told us that she had been overwhelmed with the level of stress arising from various sources. Our approach was that it was imperative that she looked after herself first before she tried to tackle her children's behaviour problems. If her emotional state remained as it was, she would have a very difficult job in bringing about any changes in the way she dealt with Brandon. If anything, when she was feeling low, she was likely to reinforce his inappropriate patterns of behaviours.

Additionally, when parents feel under stress they often become more negative in their approach in dealing with children which simply escalates behaviour problems (Cunningham & Boyle, 2002). In view of this, our main emphasis in our second session was to offer her advice as to how she could reduce her stress level and that in turn, without implementing any behaviour modification ideas, may have had some beneficial effect on Brandon's behaviour. Our advice included that she needed to have some psychological input for herself as well, given that she suffered from panic attacks and depression. She needed to set realistic targets for herself for the day to achieve. She needed to recognise, and accept, that some other mothers of her age who did not have the range of problems that she had might be able to achieve more than she would be able to achieve. She would waste less mental energy if she did not have this constant conflict in her own mind. Any opportunities she had, she must try to relax and ensure that she had regained some of her energy to deal with Brandon's constant demands.

Another example of the way we might deal with parental stress is to suggest that following our assessment, the parents introduced one of our pointers (e.g. do not say 'no', if you can say 'yes' or you are eventually going to end up saying 'yes'), which might make a considerable difference to their stress levels. As we have discussed this point at length in a previous chapter, suffice to say that it is an important point and it does help significantly in reducing parental stress, and this has been reported to us again and again in our clinical work.

Our clinical observations that a large number of parents feel highly stressed with the way their children behave and the manner in which they deal with them are well supported by some research evidence as well. In a survey of 1218 parents in Queensland (Australia), 63% of parents reported that parenting was very demanding; while 25% stated that it was stressful (Sanders et al., 1999). Esdaile & Greenwood (2003), based on their study of 53 mothers and 25 fathers of children with disabilities, found that their scores on the Parent Stress Index were quite high (see also Dyson, 1997). A recent study by Martin & Sanders (2003) also discovered that parents not only experience stress at home with their children's oppositional behaviours, but parenting demands can also 'spill-over between family and work life'. When children's behaviours cause stress to their parents, it adversely effects their enjoyment of the parenting role, has a negative impact on their social lives (Donenberg & Baker, 1993; Podolski & Nigg, 2001; Pukinskaite, 2002) and it can also affect their self-esteem (Johnston, 1996). In line with a common sense view, a few studies have found that different parents react differently to the stress they experience in bring up their children and sometimes there are differences between mothers and fathers in their ability to cope (Esdaile & Greenwood, 2003; Headman, 1995; Krauss, 1993; Little, 2002). Little's study of differences and similarities between mothers and fathers in their child-related stress levels found that mothers of children with Asperger's Syndrome experienced more stress related to family problems, felt more pessimistic about their children's future, required more therapy, and used more antidepressants than fathers. Clearly from a practical point of view, this means that clinicians cannot take it for granted that both parents are likely to experience the same level of stress from their children's behaviour.

Esdaile & Greenwood (2003) recommend that given parents' experience of stress arising from raising children with disabilities, stress management should be an integral part of their therapy programme. In our view, it is not just parents of children with disabilities who need guidance in the management of their stress levels, but all parents who feel overwhelmed in the looking after of their children per se. Furthermore, if clinicians understand parental affect and cognition, it assists in explaining, predicting, and changing parental behaviour (Grusec et al., 2000).

The role of the clinician in giving positive feedback to the child

This is the second major variable that we have introduced in our approach; that is, the role of the clinician in giving positive feedback to the child. This is done in the following way: following a child's first visit to us, we might send him a letter of the following type on letter-headed paper addressed to the child. To make the letter look attractive, we ask the child what kind of picture he would like to have on the letter. Sometimes, if we know that a child is particularly fond of something (e.g. football or some other sport, animals, cars, etc.) we may have a computer-generated picture inserted pertaining to that interest. Following are a few examples of the letters that we have sent to many children. They are designed to serve different purposes, which we will outline after we have given examples of a few letters first.

Example 1

Dear Brandon

Thank you for coming to see me today. It was nice to meet you. I must say that whilst you were here, your behaviour was very good. You were also very polite and occupied yourself very well and let your mum talk to me without any interruptions.

Best wishes.

Yours sincerely,

Clinician

Example 2

Dear Michael

Thank you for coming to see me today. It was nice to meet you and talk with you.

Thank you for agreeing to the following:

Not shouting
Not being nasty to your brother
Not to say hurtful things to your dad.

Do not forget what we agreed today.

Best wishes,

Clinician

Example 3

Dear Dean

I was very pleased to hear from your mum that you are maintaining good behaviour.

Well done. Keep it up.

Best wishes,

Clinician

Example 3A (this is a slight variant of Example 3)

Dear Callum

I was very pleased to hear from your mum today that:

You have not been smacking your mum
You do not mind going to school now
You like P.E. now

All in all, your behaviour has improved a lot.

Excellent achievement!

Keep it up!

Yours sincerely,

Clinician

Example 3B

Dear Luke

Your mum came to see me today. I was very pleased to hear from her that now you often go down on your own and also started to sleep in your own bedroom.

I think you are doing very well indeed.

Excellent Progress

Keep it up

Best wishes.

Yours sincerely,

Clinician

Example 3C

Dear Adam

Thank you for coming to see me today. I was very pleased to hear about the following improvements in your behaviour.

- You do not have as many temper tantrums as you used to have and they do not last very long now.
- You apologise when you feel you have been wrong.
- You recognise what is right and wrong.
- You are getting much better at school and do not get involved in fights.
- You are much more contented.
- You do not hit your mum.
- I was also very impressed with your clever idea of dealing with your brother.

All in all, you have made

Best wishes.

Yours sincerely,

Clinician

We have sent hundreds of letters like these; our experience is that children really like receiving such letters. In addition, they serve several other important functions that are helpful in the therapeutic outcome. In our view these letters are helpful in the following ways.

Helping building rapport with the child

In cases where a child is not very communicative during their first interview, after their first visit we send them a letter that has been produced as in Example 1 above. More often than not, when they come to see us the next time, they tend to be a little more communicative. A letter of this type seems to help break the ice between the child and the clinician. If they are still very reserved during their second visit as well, we will still send them another letter focusing on the good points during their visit and ignoring the fact that the child had been unwilling to talk. We are not claiming this approach to be a panacea for establishing a relationship with the child and that it works in all situations; it is just an additional tool which is often successful and the majority of the children respond well and value receiving personalised letters. As well as building rapport, such letters also help the clinician to be seen in a more positive light in situations where children may have some preconceived ideas about the professionals who work in services like CAMHS (particularly psychologist and psychiatrists).

Giving positive feedback

The letters produced in Example 3, 3A, and 3B are meant to serve as positive feedback from us to the child. If we have managed to build a good relationship with the child, almost always the child appreciates receiving such letters from us. In fact we ask parents to inform us if the child has displayed improved behaviour, so that we can send him another letter. This is routinely done. However, not all parents inform us on a regular basis. Sometimes, we give them a ring and check with them as to how their child is getting on. During such a call we help parents to identify if the child has done something positive, so that he can be sent one of these letters.

Providing a model of positive feedback for the parents

Many parents we see are not used to providing positive reinforcement to their children, nor is it their common experience to have a professional sending such personal letters to their children. We hope these letters act as a kind of model (see 'Modelling', p. 86) for the parents so that they learn and start providing positive feedback to the child more frequently than they have done previously when they see that their child is behaving. In other words, such letters can help parents to see the good side as well, rather than focusing on the negatives which they had been doing routinely.

Providing a reminder (prompt) to the child

We use it as a kind of reminder to the child to see that he is still doing what he agreed to do. Depending upon the situation, it can help the child initiate the agreed behaviour if he had not already done it, or maintained it, so that he can receive his agreed rewards. Letter 2 is an example which is aimed to serve that purpose.

We tend to use it when the parent has informed us over the telephone, or if they have come to see us without their child, that the child has not been behaving. Rather than saying that he has not been behaving, we use this somewhat circuitous approach to help to remind the child that he should try and remember what was agreed between him and his parents and us (see Ollendick & Cerny, 1985, which provides theoretical underpinning for prompts). Very occasionally, we might say, if the child had really behaved inappropriately, that we were disappointed to hear from his parents that he still hits his sister or younger sibling or is rude. On the whole, we try to avoid sending a child a letter which sends a critical message or has negative connotations.

Helping to revise self-concept

We think that as a result of establishing a good relationship with the child, our views conveyed through the letters (and our positive face-to-face feedback) is likely to help him revise the child's perception from being a naughty boy to a well-behaved boy (see Letter 3, as an example). The importance of self-concept and how it develops has already been discussed and, therefore, we won't go over that ground here again.

We have not done any proper trials with this approach to see if this additional factor of sending letters that we have introduced to our behaviour modification approach has any real benefit in the modification of the child's behaviour. The only claim that we can make in its support is that the majority of children and their parents have made very positive comments about it and our subjective judgement suggests that it has the benefits that we have listed above. In addition, in three different clinics, some of the psychologist colleagues of the first author adopted this approach as well. For quite a few psychologists to adopt this approach would indicate that this must have some face validity.

KEY STEPS OF BEHAVIOURAL INTERVENTION

What follows next are the three key phases which are helpful in bringing about change. These are based on learning theory and what is often termed as behaviour modification, and they have been somewhat modified here so that they are more acceptable to parents. As observed above, our experience, current practice and a survey conducted some time ago would suggest that it is perhaps this type of adapted version of behaviour modification that is actually practised and not the one which has been tried only in experimental situations (see Coxhead & Gupta, 1989; Gupta & Coxhead, 1990; Gupta & Parry-Gupta, 2003; cf. O'Connor, 2002). It is our view that this type of approach is more acceptable, realistic, and practical to parents and many of them do not put up barriers in accepting it.

Component 1

Not selecting many target behaviours

A child may display a number of behaviour problems. He could be rude, disobedient, and not work at school. It is invariably less effective if parents embark on dealing with all the behaviour excesses or deficits in one go. It is best to focus on one or two behaviours at a time. For instance, an intelligent, extremely likeable 2½-year-old girl was referred to us with sleep problems and for being a fussy eater. Her health and weight seemed satisfactory for her age. In agreement with the parents, we decided to target her sleep problem first. The main reason for targeting this behaviour was that it was causing a lot more stress to the family than her being a fussy eater.

Trying to change all the behaviours is demanding and unrealistic for the child and for the parents. It is not possible to change anybody completely overnight. Any such attempts are likely to lead to frustration and failure, on the part of the parents and of the child. When that happens, people often give up because they perceive intervention as not working. Equally important is the fact that the child is also clear about the exact nature of the behaviour expected of him and being clear about the consequences.

In order to continue to persevere to bring about change in the child's behaviour, both the child and the parents need positive feedback. The parent needs to see that as a result of their extra time and effort they are able to witness some improvement in their child's behaviour. Likewise, the child needs to notice that he is succeeding as a result of his efforts and is receiving positive feedback from his parents. When that begins to happen (i.e. both parents and children begin to succeed), it can help set in motion a kind of virtuous cycle. Thus when one target behaviour has been modified, then parents can focus their attention on another one.

While discussing this point with parents, it is well worth reminding them of some of the following factors.

1. It is always helpful when embarking upon such an approach that the behaviour selected is not entrenched, and the child has the requisite skill to perform the behaviour. A difficult and well-established behaviour is likely to require a lot more patience and effort to treat. The thing to do is to identify only one or two target behaviours to work on and which are not very ingrained.
2. When an undesirable behaviour has been eliminated almost completely, only then should they embark upon the next one. If they hasten the process, the child can regress to his old patterns of behaviour.
3. The target behaviour chosen should be realistic as well as not being too deep-rooted. A mother of a 13-year-old boy, David, used to find it highly annoying that after she returned from work, her son made demands on her. This made her very short-tempered and it set the scene for the rest of the evening and for the following day. This happened almost every day. Because it was more or less a regular occurrence, Mum carried feelings of irritation, anger, and lack of understanding against her son nearly all the time when she was at home. In view of these feelings, neither Mum nor David looked forward to seeing each other on return from work. She would return home anticipating a 'battle' with her son. The target behaviour that she wanted changing in David was that, when she returned from work, David should leave her in peace for half an hour and this would give her the opportunity of unwinding herself.

   Furthermore, instead of seeking her attention, Mum expected that he should make a cup of tea for her and let her rest before she did anything for him. Given the nature of Mum's job, she did need some rest and did need to relax before she could pay any attention to her son who had not seen his Mum since the morning. In the mornings too, he got little attention because Mum was busy doing other things.

   We have a dilemma here. On the one hand, Mum had a genuine need to unwind herself. On the other hand, it was unrealistic on the part of

David's mother to expect from him that he should appreciate her needs and give her some peace and quiet, especially when he had not seen her all day; that David should also appreciate, as she did, that she works in order to earn money to pay all the household bills. If she did not, they would not have much money. In so far as David was concerned, he did not get any attention from his mother either in the mornings or in the evenings. He got only negative attention. In our view, we did not think that David was capable of seeing things from his mother's perspective. In the light of that, our interpretation was that his mother's expectations of David were unrealistic and she needed to make some changes to ensure that she recognised her son's needs as well.

4. Having selected a realistic target behaviour, parents need to ensure that they help the child to succeed and do not make it difficult for him. For instance, sometimes parents say that a child has to behave at least for a month before he can get his reward.

While parents are working on one problem behaviour, what should they do with the other offending behaviours? First of all, some research shows that when one area improves, it has a beneficial effect on other behaviours as well (Kazdin, 1982). Secondly, the position that we have taken in this context is to advise parents that either they could carry on dealing with those other behaviours as they had been, or they could start ignoring them as much as possible. We should mention here, though, that we would never tell a parent to ignore a behaviour where a child could hurt himself or somebody else; or where the child could cause some damage to the property, e.g. to doors or to electronic equipment or anything else. Under such circumstances, parents have to intervene but in a way that they do not unwittingly reinforce his wrong patterns of behaviours. However, the important thing here is that the child should continue to receive his promised reward (for details see the next section, 'Use of rewards/reinforcement') so long as he is engaging in his agreed behaviour.

Component 2

Use of rewards/reinforcement

Often when parents are discussing how they manage their children's behaviour, a very high percentage of them list a number of punishments such as withdrawal of privileges that they have employed (cf. O'Leary & Sanderson, 1990) in order to deal with their children's unacceptable behaviours. A vast number of parents who come to see us, often report that their main modus operandi for dealing with their children's unacceptable behaviours tend to be some form of punishment, notwithstanding their being fully aware of their lack of effectiveness. If they have used rewards/ positive reinforcements (we use these two words interchangeably), many parents often have negative views about them. For instance, some parents would say that the child tried to behave until he had his reward; once he got the reward, he reverted to his old behaviours. In some cases, they say that after a week or so the child had become indifferent to rewards and could not care less about them.

Regardless of parental reservations about the use of rewards, as a general rule we subscribe to the view that rewards (whether tangible or intangible) are more effective in bringing about desirable change in the child's behaviour than punishments. In line with many academic and practising psychologists, in our clinical work we therefore place significantly more emphasis on the use of rewards with children than punishments. However, for the rewards to be effective, certain principles need to be borne in mind, which include some of the following (for an interesting perspective on the effect of praise on children's motivation, you are also referred to a paper by Henderlong & Lepper, 2002).

1. Rewards should be immediate, as far as possible. Rewards are less effective if a parent says to the child that he needs to be 'good' for a week before he can get his reward. In one case, a grandfather promised his grandson that if he were 'good' for nearly three months, he would get him a dog. When rewards are delayed for such long periods, in the majority of cases, they do not produce the results that parents want to achieve, i.e. for the child to be good for a week or months continuously before they can earn any reward. Many children are likely to find it difficult to be 'good' for a week, let alone three months, if they have not been in the habit of behaving for such a length of time. The time set should be such that the child is likely to succeed. For instance, if a parent knows that on average their child can be 'good' for about two days they should try to agree to give him a reward even before two days. Yet another important consideration for the child to be successful in getting the reward is to ensure that the target behaviour agreed with him should be unambiguous and specific both to the parent and to the child to avoid any misunderstanding between them. In other words, the child needs to be clear and to understand what he is expected to do in order to achieve the agreed reward. If the child is vague about what is expected of him, the chances are that he is unlikely to succeed in producing the desirable behaviour. All this helps to ensure that the child does succeed in getting the reward and does not fail. The receipt

of the reward is likely to help increase the frequency of the behaviour the parents want their child to demonstrate more often.

2. If conditions for getting the reward are perceived to be difficult for the child, he is likely to stop bothering to make any effort to get the reward. In other words, the child would continue to behave in the way he had been. This, in turn, would mean that parents would go back to resorting to using punishment to control behaviour, which we have all along indicated is less effective (for more details see 'Use and role of punishment', p. 124).

3. It is no good being overgenerous with rewards for a fortnight or so, and then not being able to sustain them for reasons such as expense. When Mitchell's parents first introduced a reward system they spent nearly a hundred pounds. First, Stepdad gave Mitchell ten pounds for Easter. Then, he gave him another five pounds for not mouthing and generally being well behaved. During the same period, his mother gave him five pounds and also bought him expensive rollerblades. In addition to this, he got some money and presents from other members of the family because it was Easter. If a child gets used to that level of spending on him, it is highly unlikely that he would be satisfied with less. For a very large number of families, it is almost impossible to spend that amount of money on one child only, if one has to maintain it over a period of time.

4. Rewards do not need to be expensive. If a parent gives rewards which are expensive they cannot consistently maintain giving such a present each time their child shows desirable behaviour – obviously, over a long period of time, they won't be able to afford them. One of our parents did a very clever thing in managing to buy little toys for his stepdaughter quite cheaply. This father bought loads of dolls' furniture from a boot sale at a very cheap price. Whenever his stepdaughter showed desirable behaviour, out came the reward, which he had quietly tucked away to ensure that his stepdaughter did not know that he had loads of those toys hidden away. If possible, it is best that the child does not know that the rewards are hidden away in the house. If a child knows that they are there, it is likely to be tempting for the child to keep on asking for more.

5. It is vitally important that the child must like the agreed rewards. It is no good for parents to think that the child *ought* to like them. It is the child who decides about the likes or dislikes of the reward. It should be respected and within reason accepted, provided of course parents can afford it. However, even if a child initially suggests a reward, which is quite expensive, it can often be negotiated with the child so that they can come up with an alternative, which is within the parents' price range and is acceptable to both the parties. We can recall a situation

where the mother could afford only 10 pence per day towards the reward that her 14-year-old daughter wanted (this was back in 1990), although, even then, it was a very small sum. This girl, however, agreed to accept that amount quite gracefully and happily.

6. Sometimes parents are tempted to stop rewarding even for those behaviours where it was agreed with the child and when the child is showing some improvement. This happens where the child presents a number of behaviour problems: whilst there is clearly an improvement in the agreed behaviour, but not in the other areas. Take for instance, a child hits his mother when angry, is rude to his teachers in school and is a fussy eater. Following a discussion with the clinician, parents and the child agreed that if he did not hit his mother he would earn a reward. Say the child stops doing that whilst still engaging in his other unacceptable behaviours: such as being a finicky eater and being generally rude to teachers. Because of this, the parents can be tempted to stop rewarding his behaviour where he is showing some improvement. This temptation, though understandable, should be avoided, and the child should continue to be rewarded so long as he maintains improvement in the agreed behaviour. Once that behaviour has been improved, and there is little chance of regression, then the next behaviour can be targeted and so on.

7. Sometimes parents stop giving the agreed reward because they feel that they have spent a lot of money in other areas for the child. That may well be the case. Our advice to parents has always been that they must stick to the agreed reward and they do not have to spend their money on the other stuff. Benjamin's mother stopped giving him the agreed reward of 50 pence per day for his desirable behaviour because she said that she had been buying him other things. Benjamin did not consider the other things that his mother bought for him as a reward. The agreed reward was 50 pence which he felt was not given to him. Thus, although in this case his mother spent a lot more money, it was not perceived as a reward by Benjamin and thus had little effect on his behaviour.

Advantages of using rewards

We outline below some of the advantages of using rewards as opposed to sanctions, which many parents are more inclined to use when their children do not behave the way they want them to behave.

1. The biggest advantage of using rewards, as has already been stated above, is that, on the whole, they are much more effective in bringing

about change in the child's behaviours than various forms of sanctions and withdrawal of privileges.

2. Another significant gain is that the use of rewards does not carry all the associated disadvantages of using punishments, which have been outlined below. When rewards are appropriately used, they help the child appreciate what is expected of him, and they also realise that effort involved in producing desirable behaviour was worthwhile because it is followed by pleasing consequences.

3. Children feel positively about their parents and rewards help develop better relationships between parents and children. In our view, this strength of relationship is *exceedingly* important, just as it is between the client and the therapist. Just as the therapist uses strategies to establish a good relationship with the client, likewise the parent needs to do the same thing. It just does not happen on its own and without taking positive steps. The use of rewards goes some way to achieving that goal. It has already been underscored that it is very important that children do not develop a negative view of their parents. When that happens, children stop caring about the relationship with their parents and then it becomes very difficult to modify children's behaviour. There is some evidence (e.g. Pettit, Bates & Dodge, 1997) which suggests that parents who tend to be more positive (rewarding) to the child reduce/prevent the risk of their children developing conduct disorder.

Examples of the way rewards could be used

Outlined below are some of the possible ways that rewards should be used.

1. When a child is engaged in a desirable behaviour, behaviour that a parent wants his child to demonstrate more often, it is imperative that it is reinforced with a small reward/praise/attention. It is very tempting for a parent to ignore the child when he is busy and not causing any problems, and to carry on with the jobs they have to do. Erroneously, they can be tempted to think that it is a good opportunity for them to get on and complete their chores, while their child is busy with what he is doing. But such behaviour on the part of the parent, while understandable, is unlikely to teach the child that when he behaves, he gets attention/reward and that it is in his interest to carry on engaging in such behaviour (see also Manassis & Young, 2001, who look at the ways of adapting reward systems for children who present 'extremes' of temperament, e.g. temperamentally rigid, sensation seeking, and negativistic children).

2. Rewards need to be given repeatedly and consistently over a period of time. Some parents at times expect – and say – that if they had rewarded their child once, its effect should last for a long time. For instance, if they had gone shopping and they had bought their child some sweets or a small toy, some parents start expecting that the child should continue to behave even if they pay him no more attention and irrespective of how much time they spend on shopping.

Resistance to implementing rewards system

Sometimes there are occasions, this can happen with both parents and teachers, when they reject any suggestion of rewards on the basis of their principles and belief system. Essentially, they regard rewards as bribery and their expectation is that the child ought to be able to behave without any rewards. If after describing all the benefits of the reward system, these people still adhere to their views, we have no choice but to accept their position and explain the limitations of working without the use of rewards. We can recount what seems to us a very interesting situation, where parents point blank refused to provide their child with a reward, which in our view had an adverse effect on the child.

In previous pages, we have referred to Ryan's case. As noted earlier, he really started to show significant improvement in his behaviour and keeping out of criminal activities. The improvement which Ryan showed far exceeded what we had expected when we first discussed his case with his mother, and then with his father. During our consultations with Ryan, we asked him that given that he had showed such an improvement, what reward he would like to help him to maintain that type of behaviour. He very emphatically said that he would love a monkey bike. He was aware that they were expensive. In view of this he said that he would be very happy with a secondhand one and also he was happy to have it as a joint Christmas and birthday present from all the members of his family. In a way, it would seem that he was trying to emulate his father who was interested in motorbikes. Unfortunately, his father firmly said that in no way was he going to have one, notwithstanding a significant improvement in his conduct disorder behaviour. Despite our extremely strong recommendation to his father that he should try and get it for him, he dismissed it completely by saying that Ryan was using us for his own ends and even stopped coming to see us. There was nothing that we could do, under the circumstances, except to carry on working with Ryan, given that lack of parental support made not only the situation difficult but also made his progress erratic and slow.

In summary, the use of rewards so that they are helpful in bringing about desirable changes is more complex than many parents may think and they need to be made aware of it. This is particularly important in situations where parents have seen a professional before and they introduced the rewards system, not taking into account some of its key aspects which have been outlined above. When the use of rewards is suggested to such parents, their initial response can be that they have tried them and they do not work. Such parents need to be convinced that when rewards are used appropriately they do help in bringing about desirable change even in situations which may appear hopeless to parents.

Component 3

Use and role of punishment

A textbook definition of punishment is: 'A procedure used to decrease the strength of a response by presenting an aversive stimulus whenever the response occurs' (Atkinson et al., 1990, p. A20). For our purpose here, we will define punishment as a signal or a message (verbal or non-verbal) given by the parents to the child following a behaviour of which they disapprove, and that they want him to stop. The behaviour could be not putting his shoes away when asked; the punishment could be parents shouting. The behaviour of a 16-year-old boy could be coming home drunk and much later than the parents said the adolescent boy should be back, and the punishment could be being 'grounded' for weeks or for a shorter period, depending upon the parents' habit of administering the level of punishment.

Different parents use different types and different levels of punishments, when they want to convey their disapproval of their child's behaviour. A parent may remove the plug when the child consistently plays music very loud. Another parent may refuse to buy CDs; yet another parent may resort to shouting or smacking and so on. Not only do parents use different types of punishments, the severity also varies considerably. With some parents a minor departure from acceptable behaviour may incur parents' serious wrath. Sometimes there are significant differences between parents in the amount of punishment they administer. One parent may be laid-back and may require a lot of annoyance before they give any punishment to the child. The other parent can be quick to respond and quick to administer punishment.

It is perfectly comprehensible that, when a child has been repeatedly very annoying, and doing things that parents think that he ought not to be doing, the temptation is to be punitive, and in some cases very punitive. When that happens, parents may take many privileges away from the child, as well as grounding him; or use any other punishment familiar to most of us, including physical punishment (here we are not including cases of child abuse).

Whatever levels of punishments parents use, when that amount of punishment is frequently used, children get habituated to that punishment before they respond, or stop doing what they have been asked to do. Eventually, then, even that type of punishment begins to have little effect. Punishment below that level is unlikely to make the child respond. Some children get used to responding only when they have been screamed at by their parents. Another child learns to respond only when they had a hard smack. A third child gets used to very little punishment and feels upset because his father has called him 'stupid'. Yet another child may respond to reasoning. Consider the case of a five-year-old boy with suspected Asperger's Syndrome. In school, he pulled a girl's hair and was generally somewhat aggressive towards her. When he came home, his mother tackled it in a most effective manner. She did not shout at him; she was not cross with him but said to him that she did not expect that type of behaviour from her lovely, and generally well behaved, boy. She asked him if he would play with the girl and be nice to her the next day. The boy reported to his mother that he did and since then she never heard of a further incidence of any kind of aggression towards another child.

It is not always easy for some parents to deal with that type of behaviour in the calm and composed manner shown in the above brief case history. This becomes particularly difficult where a parent, herself, received harsh treatments if she did not jump when their parents asked her to jump.

What punishment does is temporarily stop the behaviour, but it does not teach the child an alternative acceptable response. The latter should be the aim of a behaviour programme and not a temporary stop. Because a child has just temporarily stopped for fear of punishment, before long, he would revert to that type of behaviour. Parents will have to administer punishment again and possibly feel even angrier as to why the child does not learn. It is no wonder that clinicians endlessly hear from parents in the clinic situation that they had used a variety of the punishments and nothing has taught the child to behave. A situation can even arise where adolescents start threatening their parents that if they 'touched' him they would inform the social services. This was the case with Penny, who has already been mentioned on p. 7.

While punishment has a place in modifying the child's behaviour, on the whole, rewards are more effective. In fact, in 1998, the American Academy of Paediatrics came to the conclusion that 'physical discipline is of limited effectiveness and has potentially deleterious side effects and recommended that parents be encouraged and assisted in the development of methods other than spanking for managing undesirable behaviours' (cited in Lansford et al., 2004). We share this view unreservedly. However, if parents feel that they have to resort to administering punishment, it needs to be absolutely minimum. If the minimum amount does not work, it can be increased, but a sledgehammer should never be used to crack a nut in the first place. Parents need to bear in mind that if they have exhausted all their punishments, what is left if the child were to do something very serious?

Adverse consequences of punishment

Punishment may stop an undesirable behaviour temporarily, but it is considered to have several disadvantages. Some of the adverse outcomes of the punishment seen by the child as unfair, unreasonable, excessive, and unnecessary are as follows:

1. It can lead to the fear or dislike of the person (parent or teacher) and the place (school or home) where the punishment takes place. This can result in children starting to avoid parents or school, which means they will have fewer opportunities of learning acceptable ways of behaving from adults.
2. A considerable body of research shows that children behave in a non-compliant and defiant manner when their parents' interactions are very directive and negative (see Olson et al., 2002, and many studies cited therein).
3. The use of verbal aggression alone (as distinct from physical punishment) can have an adverse effect on children's self-esteem and school achievement (Solomon and Serres, 1999).
4. Children who receive more frequent smacking are likely to show more socio-emotional problems (Eamon, 2001). Eamon in her study also found that depressed mothers tend to resort to physical punishment more frequently.
5. Where the punishment is severe or painful, it may lead to even worse behaviour than the original undesirable behaviour. When severe discipline is accompanied by usually high moral standards, it can seriously repress the child and results in a child who lacks spontaneity, warmth, and who excessively worries about controlling impulses which are natural. Such children often subject themselves to severe self-recrimination and self-punishment for real and imagined mistakes and misdeeds. They may apply the same standards to the behaviour of their peers, thus earning them a reputation of being 'prudes' or worse.

6. It can result in a mistrust of others.
7. 'Severe discipline, combined with restrictiveness, may also lead to rebellion and socially deviant behaviour as children grow older and are subjected to outside influences incompatible with parental views and practices' (Carson and Butcher, 1992, p. 122; see also Leinonen et al., 2003; Lansford et al., 2004, for several studies cited therein which show an association between harsh punishment and both internalising and externalising symptoms in children).
8. Parents who use harsh punishments (which can take the form of physical punishment) are unwittingly teaching their children to be aggressive in their behaviours towards others, and may contribute to them later becoming aggressive parents (see also 'Modelling', p. 86).
9. Furthermore, harsh punitive parenting has also been found to be a risk factor in children developing conduct disorder (Dodge, Pettit & Bates, 1997; Nix et al., 1999) and becoming violent adults (Herrenkohl & Russo, 2001). Thus, sadly, they are sowing the seeds of a vicious cycle, i.e. when these children become parents, they are likely to use an excessive amount of punishment themselves on their children.

What we recommend to parents about using punishment

1. Thus, when it comes to punishment, our message has always been that it should be used absolutely minimally, or, if possible, avoided. The principle that underpins the latter approach is to reward an alternative and acceptable response. For instance, the child can be stopped from playing football in the lounge, but rewarded when he goes and plays outside. Another example could be: if one sibling is sitting and eating nicely, and the other is not, parents could try and reward/praise the former and, if possible, ignore the latter rather than nagging for not eating properly. Admittedly, there can be situations where greater ingenuity both on the part of the clinician and the parent is required to think of alternative ways of positively reinforcing acceptable responses.

Interesting evidence of the effect of using very little punishment comes from some of the societies that Margaret Mead has studied (cited in Hayes & Orrell, 1987). In one of the New Guinea tribes studied by Mead she found that people in that tribe believed that children would naturally grow into sociable and decent human beings. Unacceptable behaviours went unpunished because the people in that tribe believed that they would grow out of that type of behaviour when they grew older. Mead also noticed that although the Samoan people did not use any harsh punishments, children were not allowed to be a nuisance to others. For instance, if children cried or were difficult, they were removed from the company of adults. This was the maximum kind of punishment that Mead observed. Mead also adds that she found that the Samoan adults were stable, friendly, and well-balanced individuals. One does wonder whether an extremely limited amount of punishment may have made some significant contribution to the way their adult population turns out to be; admittedly, we do not know what other factors could have had a positive effect on their personality as well.

2. Punishment should be the last resort and not the first line of action. Parents should actively look for ways of reducing the punishment and replacing it with positive feedback. For instance, if parents had to ground their child for the whole week, if they see that during that week he has cleaned his room, parents might say to him that they were very pleased that he had tidied up his room when he was asked, and there-fore they were going to reduce his punishment to six days. If likewise they observe similar acceptable behaviour, they may further reduce it by another day and so on.

3. We think that it is important that the parents need to create an impres-sion in the mind of their children that their parents are not unduly punitive and critical. Nobody likes punishment even when they know that they are wrong. Children are likely to like it even less, if they feel they do not deserve it and are continually being punished. The weight of the pendulum should never lean towards excessive parental criticism, hostility, and punishment, as a considerable body of evi-dence has shown that these are risk factors 'for long-term outcome in child psychopathology' (see several studies cited in Bolton et al., 2003, concerning parental 'expressed emotion'). Parents have to use sanctions to discipline their children's behaviour; they need to ensure that they are also very rewarding to counterbalance the effect of negative feelings that punishment creates in the minds of their children towards their parents. In addition, parents need to be warm, sensitive, and do things with children which they find stimulating and interesting from their perspective and *not* necessarily from the parents' perspective, because sometimes what parents think should be enjoyable for the child, may not be so from the child's point of view.

This chapter concludes our therapeutic approach which we often use either in conjunction with or without the pointers that we have described in the previous two chapters. As we have stated on a few occasions in the previous pages, in our experience, and as reported by a vast number of parents, the pointers and our adapted version of behaviour modification do help children with a myriad of problems, both externalising and internalising. Furthermore, they appear to help improve the family dynamics and also assist in reducing stress on parents when they have children with a whole range of problems.

7

FROM POINTERS TO PRACTICE

EXAMPLES OF PARENTAL RESPONSES TO OUR APPROACH

We have discussed parental responses to our approach (which includes pointers and our modified behaviour modification approach) under various headings. This has been done for ease of description and is not implied that these are discrete categories, or that the list is exhaustive. For instance, there could be some commonality in the approach to our intervention by those families whom we have described as medicalising the problem, those described as putting up barriers, and those described as tending to place all the blame on the child for his problems. Before we turn to the various parental responses to our pointers, our overall impression is that, on the whole, the parents respond quite positively to our pointers and adapted behaviour modification approach, and would also appear to benefit from it. We first start outlining the response of those parents who are able to implement our advice fully.

Parents Who Implement Advice Fully

When parents do give or are able to give these ideas a fair try, the success rate is very high. This crucial point will be supported by the case of Kelly, a ten-year-old girl, whose main problem was sleeping disorder. She was referred to our service by her family doctor. Kelly had difficulty getting to sleep over the last two years. Her parents (mother 43 years old and father 33 years old) had noticed that the problem appeared to be related to the fact that the family moved to a new house and Kelly had to start sleeping alone in her bedroom. Prior to that, the family was living in a one-bedroom flat and Kelly was sleeping in the same bedroom as her parents. This was almost from birth until she was nearly seven years plus. When they came to see us Kelly's mother said that she had an interrupted sleeping pattern, had difficulty settling in her own room; she always woke up in the night to come into her parents' bedroom. They were dealing with this problem by Mum sleeping in one bedroom and Dad in another so that when Kelly woke up in the middle of the night, she went into her mother's bedroom. Obviously, the parents were not happy with this arrangement and this was causing a considerable amount of stress to the family. Kelly's mother wanted to know what was causing her to be unhappy at night and why she did not seem able to settle in her own room.

Mrs E, when she came to see us was unemployed; prior to that, she had a busy job that took her away from home for one or two nights in a week. Kelly's father was an engineer who fitted CCTV cameras. Only Mrs E and Kelly came to see us.

Kelly presented as a quiet, well-behaved and very likeable girl who enjoyed reading. She had brought a reading book to occupy herself while we were talking to her mother. She related very well and her behaviour in the clinic situation appeared age appropriate. When she was asked any questions, she gave appropriate answers. The relationship between her mother and Kelly seemed very warm and affectionate.

Mum's own hypothesis about the problem was that possibly it was the length of time they lived in a one-bedroom flat and Kelly got used to her parents being in the same bedroom. We found Mrs E's hypothesis quite appealing and conveyed to her that we agreed with her. The following is a summary of the advice given to her:

- Before going to bed, if Kelly wanted her mother to go with her, she would go with Kelly *happily*. Her mother's willingness to go happily was emphasised.
- Parents should also make absolutely clear to her that if she woke up in the middle of the night, she was *welcome* to come to her parents' bedroom. She should not feel anxious or guilty about going into her parents' bedroom. Unlike some parents, these parents did not object to Kelly coming into their bedroom. We would not recommend this to parents who feel strongly that children should not be allowed to go into their parents' bedroom.
- Based on our previous experience of dealing with such problems, we were able to say quite emphatically to her that if our advice were implemented, the problem would go away.

After the first consultation, the following letter was sent:

Dear Kelly

Thank you for coming to see us today. We must say that we were very impressed with your reading ability and your good manners. We are confident that before long your problem will go away.

Best wishes.
Yours sincerely,

Clinician

Kelly and her mother came to see us after about two months. The mother said that she had implemented the advice which was given and that Kelly had managed to sleep in her own bedroom for the last two weeks. The key management points discussed during the session included not only going over the points raised during the first interview but also emphasising those points, as well as the use of rewards and the possibility of regression.

After this visit another letter to Kelly was sent, the contents of which are reproduced below.

Dear Kelly

Tremendous achievement

Keep it up

Yours sincerely,

Clinician

Kelly's problems did go away. She maintained progress without any regression and was eventually discharged.

A second example is the case of Brady, which has previously been mentioned. You may recall that his main problems were defiant behaviour and migraine-type headaches. Both his parents worked and came home tired and stressed. From the other details of the case given to us by his parents, our hypothesis was that parents had unrealistic expectations that were not in accord with his age, ability, and general development. We also felt that they said 'no' to Brady's demands frequently and unreasonably when they could have said 'yes' easily. So our advice was to implement one of the pointers (which is, parents should not say 'no' if they can say 'yes'; or, if they think that eventually they might end up saying 'yes', they should not say 'no' in the first place) which we have strongly recommended to parents on innumerable occasions, and which has been shown to be very helpful in reducing avoidable conflict between children and parents. In addition, we also explained the importance of having realistic demands and how when parents make unrealistic demands on their children, it can lead to so many problems between them.

When parents came back for the second session, they said that when they went home after the first session, they mocked at the idea of saying 'yes' instead of 'no' when they could (for details of this pointer please refer to Chapter 4 where we discuss this at some considerable length). For these parents, the idea of saying 'yes' when they could did not have much face validity. Notwithstanding their initial reservations, which they did not betray during the time of their first visit, they still implemented it. They were amazed at the positive effect it had on Brady's behaviour and their interactions with him became far less stressful compared to what they used to be before.

The above two cases are intended to highlight the importance of putting into action the advice which is given in the form of pointers and a kind of evidence that these pointers are helpful in bringing about change as we have been claiming in this book. Parents who implement the advice often seem to have the ability to be able to see their own shortcomings in their interactions with their children, are open to change, and willing to implement the advice given.

Parents Who Put Up Barriers

The converse has been observed as well on a number of occasions; fortunately, though, not in many cases. That is, there are parents who are not willing to put into practice the advice given. Whatever is recommended or suggested to such parents is always challenged, or rejected, or, for some reason, they are not able to apply them. Thus, while they come and see you, some even quite regularly, they still carry on treating their child as they had been doing prior to coming and consulting you. In such cases, parents should not expect any improvement in the problems which they experience with their children. Obviously, with such parents, the advice embodied in these points is least effective.

We are inclined to think that although clinicians are not infallible, it is not due to the fault of the pointers but often because of parents' inability to implement them for various reasons which have been summarised below. (This statement is made not in the spirit of criticism of the families but more as a form of observation from having worked with them over a long period.) This is not just our experience but the experience of a number of other colleagues with whom we have discussed this problem and with other therapeutic approaches as well. For instance, in Brief Solution Focused Therapy (as described by Lethem, 2002), the concept of resistance is raised, and considered unhelpful, as we are noting here. We hope that some clinicians through their expertise may be able to discover some ways to engage such clients in therapy, though this is by no means an easy task.

To illustrate this point, for ready reference, we will briefly restate the case of Jason which has been mentioned previously, as well. You may recall that his parents were seen first by a clinical psychiatric nurse (CPN) for nearly 11 months. The parents attended their appointments almost regularly. This CPN colleague tried to help them to recognise that in order to bring about any change in Jason's behaviour they needed to modify their parenting style. Jason's behavioural difficulties were essentially at home and they appeared to be a response to the way they treated him. In other contexts, including in the clinic, his behaviour was more than satisfactory. Although these parents attended therapy sessions they never put into practice any advice given because they were convinced that something was psychiatrically 'wrong' with him. Because of their dissatisfaction with the CPN's input, we were asked to see them. They attended a few sessions with us and again politely said to us that they would like to see a psychiatrist to rule out that nothing was psychiatrically 'wrong' with their son. Given their insistence, they were referred to a psychiatrist colleague.

In cases where parents continue to put up resistance to implement our advice and to change their approach towards their children, sometimes we have managed to persuade children to show some improvement *first* before a parent is willing to introduce any changes in their own behaviour towards their children. Trying to bring change in the child first does not happen very often but it occurs only in those situations where it is possible to establish a *good* therapeutic alliance with the child. For instance, we agree with the referred child that he would try and not start a fight with his younger brother. If the younger brother starts a fight with the older brother (the referred child), instead of retaliating, which he did prior to coming to see us, the older brother goes and tells his parents. Another situation could be the child agreeing with us that he would not swear or hit his mother. Should the child succeed in doing that, we have observed that sometimes this leads to parents changing their behaviour and attitude towards their children and readiness on their part to reward desirable behaviours. However it is worth noting that 'demonstrating the modifiability of children's behaviour in response to a parenting intervention does not necessarily mean that children's behavioural problems had their *origins* in disturbed parenting' (Bell & Harper, 1977, cited in O'Connor, 2002, p. 560). To this we will add that the obverse is equally true as well. In other words, if a parent changes his behaviour following changes in his child's behaviour first, it does not necessarily follow that the 'origins' of faulty interactions between the child and the parents lay with the child.

Horrendously Complex Cases

Clinicians from their experience would know that some cases are so awfully complex and, on top of that, some parents have their own personal problems, as well. This is certainly the case where there is mental illness. We can recall the case of a four-year-old boy whose parents were in their late forties. Mother had bipolar disorder and father had suffered from depression for years and from diabetes. Both parents were very loving but their personal chronic problems made it virtually impossible for them to change and implement the advice given and change their management style. In this case, hardly anything changed. In our view, it is not the case of putting up barriers as the previous case history shows, but that the family was caught in awful and extremely sad circumstances. Notwithstanding their best intentions such families find it extremely difficult to introduce any advice given consistently, though no fault of their own. In this situation, not only did our pointers make little difference to their problems, we would assume that any therapeutic intervention would have been unsuccessful in their circumstances.

Parents Who are Inconsistent

There are cases where parents with the best will in the world are inconsistent in implementing the advice given. It is not that they do not take the advice seriously; we think what perhaps happens with such parents is that when they come and see the therapist they are quite enthusiastic. They go away and put into practice the advice given for short periods, and then regress to their previous ways of dealings with the problems. When they implement the advice, they see improvement, which is reported to the clinician when they are seen next time. It then almost seems that the situation has improved to such an extent that they hardly ever see the therapist on a regular basis and they go on the therapist's review list. Under these conditions the gap between appointments is often bigger. The next time they come and see the therapist, the situation has almost regressed back to the original circumstances and one has to start all over again because they had stopped implementing the advice given, although they think they had not.

Gary's case illustrates this scenario quite well. Gary, when he was born, had serious medical complications. All his life, he was in and out of hospitals. Our view was that because of his early history of serious medical conditions, and a real question mark as to whether he was going to survive, his parents often gave in to both his reasonable and his unreasonable demands, even if he only mildly persisted. Thus, at the age of around seven years when the family came to see us, he had learnt that if he said hurtful things to his mother and persisted determinedly, he got what he wanted. His behaviour in school and when he was with his grandparents (particularly when he was with his granddad, who was laid-back and kept him occupied) was satisfactory. His mother appeared under a lot of stress with his behaviour when she saw that he was behaving inappropriately. Gary's problems also started to have an adverse effect on the parents' marital relationship. The advice was given that they needed to ignore trivial behaviours, reward desirable behaviours, both parents needed to be consistent in their approach and they must follow through if they asked him to do anything. His mother came and saw us for more than two years and because of her inconsistent use of the advice given, sometimes Gary's behaviour was satisfactory and sometimes he regressed to his old ways just as his mother returned to her old patterns of responding to him. Given his lack of consistent improvement, his mother felt that he perhaps needed some medication. Despite our reservations about this course, to comply with his mother's wishes, he was referred to a psychiatrist colleague.

We do not think that in this case, our pointers were ineffective. We attribute Gary's lack of consistent improvement to his mother's inability to put into practice the advice given. Although we saw her for more than two years, we were unable to form any reliable hypotheses as to why his mother became complacent or failed to implement consistently the advice given.

Effect of Parents' Own Upbringing

These pointers are particularly difficult for those parents who are set in their own ways of dealing with their children's undesirable behaviours, and had quite Victorian upbringings. Michael's father (Robert) very poignantly said to us that he did not know how to show love to his 14-year-old stepson. Robert never experienced any affection and warmth from his own father as a child. The interactions between Robert and his own father comprised of the latter invariably shouting at Robert. The expectation on the part of Robert's father was that when Robert was asked to 'jump' he should 'jump' without questioning. If Robert did not, he got the belt. It does not mean that all the parents follow their own parents' way of dealing with bad behaviour or not being able to show any love and affection. In fact some can adopt a totally opposite style to their own parents. Michael's mother was a good example of that. When Robert used to talk about his own upbringing, his wife, Caroline, used to say that her upbringing was no different from her husband's. However, she decided to reject her parents' rather authoritarian parenting style and adopted a more child-centred, more emotionally involved approach with her children and she was far more accepting of their unacceptable behaviours. Likewise, Mrs M (parent of Andrew and Scott) said that although she was both physically and sexually abused by her father, she wanted to make sure that she provided the most loving and caring environment for her children. What this illustrates is simply that different parents can react differently towards their own children depending upon their own upbringing. Irrespective of their personal experiences, when such parents put into action, consistently, advice given (i.e. the pointers) they do help these parents. In fact, in the above two situations, our help given based on some of the pointers and the adapted behaviour modification did bring about significant change.

CONCLUDING REMARKS

Our somewhat bold claims, that our pointers and our adapted behaviour modification are effective, and that the approach is less prone to parents putting up barriers and rejecting the treatment, are based on parental, and sometimes on children's, reports, on our own observations, and not on the basis of any thorough empirical evidence, a point that has been made in the Preface as well. Notwithstanding that the observational therapeutic approaches obviously lack experimental rigour, we subscribe to the view that such studies have some merit and deserve a place in clinical work. In this context, Pine (2005), in a recent editorial in the *Journal of Child*

Psychology and Psychiatry (JCPP), makes the following supportive comments about the usefulness of observational studies, while also emphasising the importance of experimental therapeutic research. Pine (2005) states that:

> Like many forums in the clinical sciences, the JCPP typically presents more results from observational than experimental therapeutic studies. Results from observational studies, no matter how rigorously executed, generate more definitive conclusions concerning mechanisms of disease when the results are extended in experimental studies . . . Because research on experimental therapeutics is extremely difficult and costly, one can reasonably ask if the effort required is too great. Might we learn just as much from observational studies that assess changes in symptoms longitudinally following potentially harmful or therapeutic events? Clearly, observational studies provide crucial insights concerning mechanisms that produce mental illness (p. 449).

It would seem that, in the main, following the implementation of pointers and adapted behaviour modification, when parents do change the way they interact with their children, they witness corresponding improvement in their children as well. Our approach encourages parents to be warm, less punitive, supportive, rewarding, empathetic, flexible, and sensitive to the child's needs, to be realistic in their expectations and demands (O'Connor, 2002, and several studies cited therein). When this begins to happen routinely, and over a period of time, not only do they see changes in their child's behaviour but also substantially reduced stress in the family dynamics.

REFERENCES

Abram RS & Coie JD (1981) Maternal reactions to problem behaviours and ordinal position of child. *J. Pers.* 49(4): 450–67.

Antshel KM, Brewster S & Waisbren SE (2004) Child and parent attributions in chronic paediatric conditions: phenylketonuria (PKU) as an exemplar. *Journal of Child Psychology and Psychiatry* 45(3): 622–8.

Atkinson RL, Atkinson RC, Smith EE, Bem DJ & Hilgard ER (1990) *Introduction to Psychology*. San Diego: Harcourt Brace Jovanovich, Publishers.

Aunola K, Nurmi JE, Onatsu-Arvilommi T & Pulkkinen L (1999) The role of parents' self-esteem, mastery orientation and social background in their parenting styles. *Scand. J. Psychol.* 40(4): 307–17.

Bandura A (1977a) *Social Learning Theory*. Englewood Cliffs: Prentice Hall.

Bandura A (1977b) Self-efficacy: toward a unifying theory of behavioral change. *Psychological Review* 84: 191–215.

Baumrind D (1967) Child care practices anteceding three patterns of preschool behaviour. *Genetic Psychology Monograph* 75: 43–58.

Baumrind D (1980) New directions in socialisation research. *Psychological Bulletin* 35: 639–52.

Baumrind D (1991) The influence of parenting style on adolescent competent and substance use. *Journal of Early Adolescence* 11(1): 56–95.

Bell RQ (1979) Parent, child, and reciprocal influences. *American Psychologist* 34: 821–6.

Berg-Nielsen TS, Vika A & Dahl AA (2003) Specific parenting problems when adolescents have emotional and behavioural disorders. *Nord. J. Psychiatry* 57: 139–46.

Blinder D, Rotenberg L, Peleg M & Taicher S (2001) Patient compliance to instructions after oral surgical procedures. *Int. J. Oral. Maxillofac. Surg.* 30: 216–19.

Bolton C et al. (2003) Expressed emotion, attributions and depression in mothers of children with problem behaviour. *Journal of Child Psychology and Psychiatry* 44(2): 242–54.

Bright M (2004) Most 'problem kids' go on thrive. *The Observer*, 13 June, p. 2.

Bryan T & Nelson C (1994) Doing homework: perspectives of elementary and middle school students. *Journal of Learning Disability* 27: 488–99.

Buchanan A, Flouri E & Ten Brinke J (2002) Emotional and behavioural problems in childhood and distress in adult life: risk and protective factors. *Aust. N.Z. J. Psychiatry* 36(4): 521–7.

Bugental BD & Johnston C (2000) Parental and child cognitions in the context of the family. *Annu. Rev. Psychol.* 51: 315–44.

Burt KB, Hay DF, Pawlby S, Harold G & Sharp D (2004) Parent-child dyadic mutuality and child behaviour problems: an investigation of gene-environment processes. *Journal of Child Psychology and Psychiatry* 45(6): 1159–70.

Calkins SD (1994) Origins and outcomes of individual differences in emotion regulation. In NA Fox (ed) *The Development of Emotion Regulation: Biological and Behavioural Considerations* (pp. 53–72). Monographs of the Society for Research in Child Development 59: Nos. 1–2.

Campbell S (1979) Mother–infant interaction as a function of maternal ratings of temperament. *Child Psychiatry and Human Development* 10: 67–76.

Campbell SB, Shaw DS & Gilliom M (2000) Early externalising behaviour problems: toddlers and preschoolers at risk for later maladjustment. *Development and Psychopathology* 12(3): 467–88.

Carnegie D (2001) *How to Win Friends and Influence People.* London: Vermilion.

Carson RC & Butcher JN (1992) *Abnormal Psychology and Modern Life.* 9th edn. NY: Harper Collins Publishers.

Chess S & Thomas A (1999) *Goodness of Fit: Clinical Applications from Infancy through Life.* Philadelphia: Brunner/Manzel.

Chess S, Thomas A & Birch MG (1965) *Your Child is a Person.* New York: Viking.

Clarke D (1996) Social cognition. In MC Cardwell, L Clark & C Meldrum (eds) *Psychology for A Level.* London: Collins.

Connor-Smith JK & Weisz JR (2003) Applying treatment outcome research in clinical practice: techniques for adopting interventions to the real world. *Child and Adolescent Mental Health* 8(1): 3–10.

Cooley CH (1902) *Human Nature and the Social Order.* New York: Charles Scribner's & Sons.

Coopersmith S (1967) *The Antecedents of Self-esteem.* San Francisco: Freeman.

Cote S, Tremblay RE, Nagin D, Zoccolillo M & Vitaro F (2002) The development of impulsivity, fearfulness, and helpfulness during childhood: patterns of consistency and change in the trajectories of boys and girls. *Journal of Child Psychology and Psychiatry* 43(5): 609–18.

Coxhead P & Gupta RM (1989) A survey of educational psychologists' views of the delivery of behaviour modification. *Educational Studies* 15: 1.

Crnic K & Acevedo M (1995) Everyday stresses and parenting. In MH Bornstein (ed) *Handbook of Parenting.* Vol. 4. Mahwah, NJ: Lawrence Erlbaum Associates.

Cumberbatch G & Humphreys P (2000) Social psychology. In D Gupta & R Gupta (eds) *Psychology for Psychiatrists.* London: Whurr.

Cunningham CE & Boyle MH (2002) Preschoolers at risk for attention-deficit hyperactivity discord and oppositional defiant disorder: family, parenting, and behavioural correlates. *Journal of Abnormal Child Psychology* 30(6): 555–69.

d'Ardenne P & Mahtani A (1999) *Transcultural Counselling in Action.* London: Sage Publications.

Deater-Deckard K & Bullock BM (2003) Gene-environment transactions and family processes: implications for clinical research and practice. In R Denham et al. (2002) Preschool understanding of emotions: contributions to classroom anger and aggression. *Journal of Child Psychology and Psychiatry* 43(7): 901–16.

Deater-Deckard K, Dodge KA, Bates JE & Pettit GS (1996) Physical discipline among African American and European American mothers: links to children's externalising behaviours. *Developmental Psychology* 32: 1065–72.

Deater-Deckard K & Petrill SA (2004) Parent–child dyadic mutuality and child behaviour problems: an investigation of gene-environment process. *Journal of Child Psychology and Psychiatry* 45(6): 1171–9.

Dekovic M & Meeus W (1997) Peer relations in adolescents: effects of parenting and adolescents' self-concept. *J. Adolesc.* 20(20): 163–76.

Denham SA, Workman E, Cole PM, Weissbrod C, Kensziora KT & Zahan-Waxler C (2000) Prediction of externalising behaviour problems from early to middle childhood: the role of parental socialisation and emotion expression. *Development and Psychopathology* 12: 23–45.

Denham SA, Caverly S, Scmidt M, Blair K, De Mulder E, Caal S, Hawada S & Mason T (2000b) Preschool understanding of emotions: contributions to classroom anger and aggression. *Journal of Child Psychology and Psychiatry* 43(7): 901–16.

Dix T (1993) Attributing dispositions to children: an interactional analysis of attributions in socialisation. *Pers. Soc. Psychol. Bull.* 19: 633–43.

Dix T, Reinhold DP & Zambarano RJ (1990) Mother's judgements in moments of anger. *Merrill-Palmer Q.* 36: 465–86.

Dix T, Ruble DN, Grusec JE & Nixon S (1986) Social cognition in parents: inferential and affective reactions to children of three age levels. *Child Development* 57: 879–94.

Dodge KA, Pettit GS & Bates GE (1997) How the experience of early physical abuse leads children to become chronically aggressive. In D Cicchetti & S Toth (eds) *Rochester Symposium of Developmental Psychopathology*. Vol. 8. Rochester, NY: University of Rochester Press.

Donenberg G & Baker BL (1993) The impact of young children with externalising behaviours on their families. *Journal of Abnormal Child Psychology* 21(2): 179–98.

Dyson LL (1997) Fathers and mothers of school age children with developmental disabilities: parental stress, family functioning, and social support. *American Journal of Mental Retardation* 102(3): 267–79.

Eamon MK (2001) Antecedents and socio-emotional consequences of physical punishment on children in two parent families. *Child Abuse and Neglect* 25: 787–802.

Eisenman R (1992) Birth order, development and personality. *Acta. Paedopsychiatr.* 55(1): 25–7.

Esdaile SA & Greenwood KM (2003) Comparison of mothers' and fathers' experience of parenting stress and attributions from parent child interaction outcomes. *Occupational Therapy International* 10(2): 115–26.

Faber A & Mazlish E (2001) *How to Talk So Kids Will Listen and Listen So Kids Will Talk*. London: Piccadilly Press Ltd.

Flavell JH (1970a) *The Developmental Psychology of Jean Piaget*. New York: Van Nostrand Reinhold Co.

Flavell JH (1970b) Developmental studies of mediated memory. In HW Reese & LP Lipsett (eds) *Advances in Child Development and Behavior*, Vol. 5. New York: Academic Press.

Fowler R (2003) The damaged generation. *Sunday Times*, 7 September, p. 4.9.

Gajria M & Salend SJ (1995) Homework practices of students with and without learning disabilities. *J. Learn. Disabil.* 28(5): 291–6.

Galboda-Liyanage KC, Prince J & Scott S (2003) Mother-child joint activity and behaviour problems of pre-school children. *Journal of Child Psychology and Psychiatry* 44(7): 1037–48.

Gardner FE, Sonuga-Barke EJ & Syal K (1999) Parents anticipating misbehaviour: an observational study of strategies parents use to prevent conflict with behaviour problem children. *Journal of Child Psychology and Psychiatry* 40: 1185–96.

Gelfand DM & Hartmann DP (1975) *Child Behaviour: Analysis and Therapy.* New York: Pergamon Press.

Gerull FC & Rapee RM (2002) Mother knows best: effects of maternal modeling on the acquisition of fear and avoidance behaviour in toddlers. *Behav. Res. Ther.* 40(3): 279–87.

Goleman D (1996) *Emotional Intelligence: Why It Can Matter More than IQ.* London: Bloomsbury.

Goodwin Y (2000) Do they listen? A review of information retained by patients following consent for reduction mammoplasty. *Br. J. Plas. Surg.* 53: 121–5.

Gottman JM, Katz LF & Hooven C (1997) *Meta-emotions: How Families Communicate Emotionally.* New Jersey: Lawrence Erlbaum Associates Inc.

Graham H (2000) Human development. In D Gupta & R Gupta (eds) *Psychology for Psychiatrists.* London: Whurr Publishers.

Greenough WT (2003) Experience effects on brain development: possible contributions to psychopathology. *Journal of Child Psychology and Psychiatry* 44: 33–63.

Gretarsson SJ & Gelfand DM (1988) Mothers' attributions regarding their children's social behaviour and personality characteristics. *Developmental Psychology* 24: 264–9.

Grossman AW, Churchill JD, McKinney BC, Kodish IA, Otte SL, Grusec JE, Goodnow JJ & Kuczynske L (2003) New directions in analyses of parenting contributions to children's acquisition of values. *Child Development* 71: 205–11.

Grusec JE & Kuczynski L (eds) (1977) *Handbook of Parenting and the Transmission of Values.* New York: Wiley.

Gupta RM (1975) A comparative study of the self concepts of West Indian and English children in Nottingham. Unpublished M.Ed. dissertation submitted to University of Manchester.

Gupta RM (1983) The assessment of the learning efficiency of Asian children. Unpublished Ph.D. thesis, The University of Aston in Birmingham.

Gupta RM & Coxhead P (eds) (1990) *Intervention with Children.* London: Routledge.

Gupta RM & Gupta J (1992) Fear of failure. *Special Children* 56: 17–19.

Gupta RM & Parry-Gupta DS (2003) *Children and Parents: Clinical Issues for Psychologists and Psychiatrists.* London: Whurr Publishers.

Hall CS & Lindsey G (1970) *Theories of Personality.* 2nd edn. New York: John Wiley & Sons, Inc.

Hanna E & Meltzoff AN (1993) Peer imitation in laboratory, home and day care contexts: implications for social learning and memory. *Developmental Psychology* 29: 1–12.

Harrington RC, Cartwright-Hatton S & Stein A (2002) Annotation: randomised trials. *Journal of Child Psychology and Psychiatry* 43: 6.

Hartman RH, Scott AS & Webster-Stratton C (2003) A growth curve analysis of parent training outcomes: examining the influence of child risk factors (inattention, impulsivity, and hyperactivity problems), parental and family risk factors. *Journal of Child Psychology and Psychiatry* 44: 388–98.

Hartman RH, Scott SA & Webster-Stratton (2003) A growth curve analysis of parent training outcomes: examining the influence of child risk factors (inattention, impulsivity, and hyperactivity problems), parental and family risk factors. *Journal of Child Psychology and Psychiatry* 44(3): 388–98.

Hastings RP & Beck A (2004) Review: stress intervention for parents of children with intellectual disabilities. *Journal of Child Psychology and Psychiatry* 45(8): 1338–49.

Hayes N & Orrell S (1987) *Psychology: An Introduction.* London: Longman.

Headman DJ (1995) Perceived stressors and coping strategies of parents who have children with developmental disabilities. *J. Paediatric Nursing* 10(5): 311–20.

Heathcote E (2004) Journey's end, four years after being given six months to live. *Independent on Sunday*, 6 June, p. 17.

Hebb DO (1972) *A Textbook of Psychology.* Eastbourne: WB Saunders.

Henderlong J & Lepper MR (2002) The effect of praise on children's intrinsic motivation: a review and synthesis. *Psychological Bulletin* 128(5): 774–95.

Herbert M (1994) *Clinical Child Psychology: Social Learning, Development and Behaviour.* Chichester: John Wiley & Sons.

Herrenkohl RC & Russo MJ (2001) Abusive early rearing and early childhood aggression. *Child Maltreatment* 6(1): 3–16.

Hill A (2003) How birth order shapes our fate. *Observer*, 31 August, p. 13.

Hinsliff G (2004) Baby, What Shall I Do? *Observer*, 9 May.

Hoffenaar PJ & Hoeksma JB (2002) The structure of oppositionality: response dispositions and situational aspects. *Journal of Child Psychology and Psychiatry* 43(3): 375–85.

Hopkins HR & Klein HA (1993) Multidimensional self-perception: linkages to parental nurturance. *Journal of Genetic Psychology* 154: 465–74.

Hotopf M, Churchill R & Lewis G (1999) Pragmatic randomised controlled trials in psychiatry. *British Journal of Psychiatry* 175: 217–23.

Huesmann LR, Eron LD & Dubow EF (2002) Childhood predictors of adult criminality: are all risk factors reflected in childhood aggressiveness? *Criminal Behaviour Mental Health* 12(3): 185–208.

Hurlock EB (1964) *Child Development.* 4th edn. New York: McGraw-Hill Co.

Hyman IA & Lally D (1982) A study of staff development programs for improving school discipline. *Urban Review* 14(3): 181–96.

Jenson WR, Sheridan SM, Olympia D & Andrews D (1994) Homework and students with learning disabilities and behaviour disorders: a practical, parent based approach. *J. Learn. Disabil.* 27(9): 538–48.

Jersild AT (1952) *In Search of Self.* Columbia: New York Teachers College.

Johnston C (1996) Parent characteristics and parent child interactions in families of nonproblem children and ADHD children with higher and low levels of oppositional-defiant behaviour. *Journal of Abnormal Child Psychology* 24(1): 85–104.

Joiner JE Jr & Wagner KD (1996) Parental, child centred attributions and outcome: a meta-analytic review with conceptual and methodological implications. *Journal of Abnormal Child Psychology* 24(1): 27–52.

Juffer F, Bakermans-Kranenburg MJ & Jzendoorn MH (2005) The importance of parenting in the development of disorganized attachment: evidence from a prevention study in adoptive families. *Journal of Child Psychology and Psychiatry* 46(3): 263–74.

Kagan J (1981) *The Second Year.* Cambridge, MA: Harvard University Press.

Kagan J (1997) In the beginning: the contribution of temperament to personality development. *AMPS/Modern Psychoanalysis* 22(2): 145.

Kay PJ, Fitzgerald M, Parader C & Mellencamp A (1994) Making homework work at home: the parent's perspective. *J. Learn. Disabil.* 27(9): 550–61.

Kazdin AE (1980) *Research Design in Clinical Psychology*. New York: Harper & Row.

Kazdin AE (1982) Symptom substitution, generalisation, and response covariation: implications for psychotherapy outcome. *Pschol. Bull.* 91(2): 349–65.

Kazdin AE (2002) Family and parenting interventions for conduct disorder and delinquency: a meta-analysis of randomized controlled trials. *Arch. Dis. Child.* 86(4): 251–6.

Kazdin AE (2003) Commentary. *Evidence-based Mental Health* 6(3): 81.

Kazdin AE, Holland L & Crowley M (1997) Family experience of barriers to treatment and premature termination from child therapy. *J. of Clinical and Consulting Psychology* 65(3): 453–63.

Kazdin AE & Nock MK (2003) Delineating mechanisms of change in child and adolescent therapy: methodological issues and research recommendations. *Journal of Child Psychology and Psychiatry* 44(8): 1116–29.

Kazdin AE, Siegal T & Bass D (1990) Drawing upon clinical practice to inform research on child and adolescent psychotherapy. *Professional Psychology: Research and Practice* 21: 189–98.

Kazdin AE & Wassell G (2000a) Predictors of barriers to treatment and therapeutic change in outpatient therapy for antisocial children and their families. *Mental Health Services Research* 2(1): 27–40.

Kazdin AE & Wassell G (2000b) Therapeutic changes in children, parents, and families resulting from treatment of children with conduct problems. *Journal of the American Academy of Child and Adolescent Psychiatry* 39: 414–20.

Kazdin AE & Whitley MK (2003) Treatment of parental stress to enhance therapeutic change among children referred for aggressive and antisocial behaviour. *J. Consulting Clinical Psychology* 71(3): 504–15.

Kessels RPC (2003) Patients' memory for medical information. *Journal of the Royal Society of Medicine* 96: 219–22.

Ketchum SA (1999) The relation between mothers' hostile attribution tendencies and children's externalising behaviour problems: the mediating role of mothers' harsh discipline practices. *Child Development* 70: 896–909.

Kingston L & Prior M (1995) The development of patterns of stable, transient, and school-age onset aggressive behavior in young children. *J. Am. Acad. Child Adolesc. Psychiatry* 34(3): 348–58.

Krauss MW (1993) Child-related and parenting stress: similarities and differences between mothers and fathers of children with disabilities. *American Journal of Mental Retardation* 97(4): 393–404.

Lalli JS, Casey SD & Kates K (1997) Non-contingent reinforcement as treatment for severe problem behaviour: some procedural variations. *Journal of Applied Behaviour Analysis* 30: 127–37.

Lamborn SD, Mounts NS, Steinberg L & Dornbusch SM (1991) Patterns of competence and adjustment among adolescents from authoritative, authoritarian, indulgent, and neglectful families. *Child Dev.* 62(5): 1049–65.

Lansford JE, Deater-Deckard K, Dodge KA, Bates JE & Pettit GS (2004) Ethnic differences in the link between physical discipline and later adolescent externalizing behaviours. *Journal of Child Psychology and Psychiatry* 45(4): 801–12.

Leinonen JA, Solantaus TS, Punamaki R (2003) Parental mental health and children's adjustment: the quality of marital interaction and parenting as mediating factors. *Journal of Child Psychology and Psychiatry* 44(2): 227–41.

Lethem, J (2002) Brief solution focused therapy. *Child and Adolescent Mental Health* 7(4): 189–92.

Lewis FC & Jaskir J (1983) Birth of a sibling: effect on mother–first born child interaction. *J. Dev. Behav. Pediatr.* 4(3): 190–5.

Lewis K (2003) *The Kid – A True Story.* London: Michael Joseph.

Little L (2002) Differences in stress and coping for mothers and fathers of children with Asperger's syndrome and nonverbal learning disorders. *Paediatr. Nurs.* 28(6): 565–70.

McGuire LC (1996) Remembering what the doctor said: organisation and older adults' memory for medical information. *Exp. Aging Res.* 22: 403–28.

Manassis K & Young A (2001) Adapting positive reinforcement systems to suit child temperament. *J. Am. Acad. Child Adolesc. Psychiatry* 40(5): 603–5.

Martin AJ & Sanders MR (2003) Balancing work and family: a controlled evaluation of the Triple p-positive parenting program as a work-site intervention. *Child and Adolescent Mental Health* 8(4): 161–9.

Mash EJ & Johnston CA (1982) A comparison of the mother–child interactions of younger and older hyperactive and normal children. *Child Development* 53: 1371–81.

Masters B (1993) *The Shrine of Jeffrey Dahmer.* London: Hodder & Stoughton.

Mead GH (1934) *Mind, Self and Society.* Chicago: University of Chicago Press.

Meltzoff A & Moore MK (1989) Imitation in newborn infants: exploring the range of gestures imitated and the underlying mechanisms. *Developmental Psychology* 25: 954–62.

Miller SA (1995) Parents' attributions for their children's behaviour. *Child Development* 66: 1557–84.

Morrell J & Murray L (2003) Parenting and the development of conduct disorder and hyperactive symptoms in childhood: a prospective longitudinal study from 2 months to 8 years. *Journal of Child Psychology and Psychiatry* 44(4): 489–508.

Mussen PH, Conger JJ, Kagan J & Huston AC (1990) *Child Development Personality.* 7th edn. New York: Harper & Row Publishers.

Nix RL, Pinderhughes EE, Dodge KA, Bates GE, Pettit GS & McFadyen-Ketchum SA (1999) The relation between mothers' hostile attribution tendencies and children's externalizing behavior problems: the mediating role of mothers' harsh discipline practices. *Child Development* 70: 896–909.

O'Connor TG (2002) Annotation: the effects of parenting reconsidered: findings, challenges, and applications. *Journal of Child Psychology and Psychiatry* 43(5): 555–72.

O'Leary SG & Sanderson W (1990) A survey of classrom management practices. *J. of School Psychology* 28: 257–69.

Ollendick TH & Cerny JA (1985) *Clinical Behaviour Therapy with Children.* New York: Plenum Press.

Olson SL, Bates JE, Sandy JM & Schilling EM (2002) Early developmental precursors of impulsive and inattentive behaviour: from infancy to middle childhood. *Journal of Child Psychology and Psychiatry* 43: 435–47.

Parish TS & McCluskey JJ (1992) The relationship between parenting styles and young adults' self-concepts and evaluations of parents. *Adolescence* 27(108): 915–18.

Patterson G, Reid J & Dishion T (1992) *Antisocial Boys: A Social Interactional Approach* (vol. 4). Eugene, OR: Castalia Publishing.

Pawlak JL & Klein HA (1997) Parental conflict and self-esteem: rest of the story. *J. Geet. Psychol.* 158(3): 303–13.

Pelham WE & Lang AR (1999) Can your children drive you to drink? Stress and parenting in adults interacting with children with ADHD. *Alcohol Research and Health* 23(4): 292–8.

Pettit GS, Bates GE & Dodge KA (1997) Supportive parenting, ecological context and children's adjustment: a seven-year longitudinal study. *Child Development* 68: 908–23.

Pine DS (2005) Editorial: Where have all the clinical trials gone? *Journal of Child Psychology and Psychiatry* 46(5): 449–50.

Place M, Reynolds J, Cousins A & Shelagh O'Neill (2002) Developing a resilience package for vulnerable children. *Child and Adolescent Mental Health* 7: 162–7.

Podolski CL & Nigg JT (2001) Parent stress in relation to child ADHD severity and associated child disruptive behaviour problems. *Journal of Clinical Child Psychology* 30(4): 503–13.

Pukinskaite R (2002) The impact of children with externalising difficulties on their families. *Medicina (Kaunas)* 38(4): 431–8. (The original article in Lithuanian.)

Purkey WW (1968) The search for self: evaluating student self concepts. In M Argyle & V Lee (1972) *Social Relationships*. Milton Keynes: Open University Press.

Reimers TM, Wacker DP, Derby KM & Cooper LJ (1995) Relation between parental attributions and the acceptability of behavioural treatments for their child's behaviour problems. *Behav. Disord.* 20: 171–8.

Ridley M (2003) *Nature Via Nurture: Genes, Experience and What Makes Us Human*. London: Harper Collins.

Roberts BW & DelVecchio WF (2000) The rank order consistence of personality traits from childhood to old age. *Psychological Bulletin* 126: 3–25.

Rogers C (1965) *Child-Centered Therapy*. London: Constable.

Rogers SJ, Hepburn SL, Stackhouse T & Wehner E (2003) Imitation performance in toddlers with autism and those with other developmental disorders. *Journal of Child Psychology and Psychiatry* 44(5): 763–81.

Rutter M (1980) *Changing Youth in a Changing Society*. Cambridge, MA: Harvard University Press.

Sanders MR et al. (1999) A survey of parenting practices in Queensland: implications for mental health promotion. *Health Promotion Journal of Australia* 9: 105–14.

Scott S (2003) Effective treatment conduct disorder. In RM Gupta & DS Parry-Gupta (eds) *Children and Parents: Clinical Issues for Psychologists and Psychiatrists*. London: Whurr.

Seguin JR, Arseneault L, Boulerice B, Harden PW & Tremblay RE (2002) Response perseveration in adolescent boys with stable and unstable histories of physical aggression: the role of underlying processes. *Journal of Child Psychology and Psychiatry* 43(4): 481–94.

Shiner R & Caspi A (2003) Personality differences in childhood and adolescence: measurement, development, and consequences. *Journal of Child Psychology and Psychiatry* 44(1): 20–32.

Sidebotham P (2001) Culture, stress and the parent–child relationship: a qualitative study of parents' perceptions of parenting. *Child: Care, Health and Development* 27(6): 469–85.

Slep AMS & O'Leary SG (1998) The effects of maternal attributions on parenting: an experimental analysis. *Journal of Family Psychology* 12(2): 234–43.

Solomon CR & Serres F (1999) Effects of parental verbal aggression on children's self-esteem and school marks. *Child Abuse Neglect* 23(4): 339–51.

Sputa CL & Paulson SE (1995) Birth order and family size: influences on adolescents' achievement and related parenting behaviours. *Psychol. Rep.* 76(1): 43–51.

Swann WB Jr (1996) *Self Traps: The Elusive Quest for Higher Self Esteem.* New York: Freeman.

Tharp RG & Wetzel RJ (1969) *Behaviour Modification in the Natural Environment.* New York: Academic Press.

Thomas A, Chess S & Birch HG (1968) *Temperament and Behaviour Disorders in Children.* New York: New York University Press.

Tremblay RE, Masse LC, Vitaro F & Dobkin PL (1995) The impact of friends' deviant behaviour on early onset delinquency: longitudinal data from 6 to 13 years of age. *Development and Psychopathology* 7: 649–67.

Tremblay RE et al. (1999) The search for the age of onset of physical aggression: Rousseau and Bandura revisited. *Criminal Behaviour and Mental Health* 9: 8–23.

Trent D (2000) Behaviourism and learning theory. In D Gupta & R Gupta (eds) *Psychology for Psychiatrists.* London: Whurr Publishers.

Usborne D (2004) Children left alone as parents go on strike. *Independent,* 10 November.

Vitaro F, Tremblay RE, Gagnon C & Boivin M (1992) Peer rejection from kindergarten Grade 2: outcomes, correlates, and prediction. *Merrill-Palmer Quarterly* 38: 382–400.

Wessel I, Van der Kooy P & Merckelbach H (2000) Differential recall of central peripheral details of emotional slides is not a stable phenomenon. *Memory* 8: 95–109.

Wolpe J (1958) *Psychotherapy by Reciprocal Inhibition.* Stanford: Stanford University Press.

Wolpert M (2002) *Drawing on the Evidence: Advice for Mental Health Professionals Working with Children and Adolescents.* Leicester: BPS.

Wood JJ, Mcleod BD, Sigman M, Hwang W & Chu BC (2003) Parenting and childhood anxiety: theory, empirical findings, and future directions. *Journal of Child Psychology and Psychiatry* 44(1): 134–51.

Xia G & Qian G (2001) The relationship of parenting style to self-reported mental health among two subcultures. *Journal of Adolescence* 24(2): 251–60.

INDEX